The Ultimate Healthy Snacks List

Including Healthy Snacks for adults & Healthy Snacks for kids.

Discover over 130 Healthy Snack Recipes such as Fruit Snacks, Vegetable Snacks, Healthy Snacks for Weight Loss, Fat Burning Foods, Healthy Smoothies, Quick Healthy Snacks, Healthy Sandwich Recipes, Gluten-Free Snacks & more!

By C Elias

Contents

Legal Notice:

The author and publisher of this book have used their best efforts in preparing this book. The author and publisher make no representation or warranties with respect to the accuracy, applicability, or completeness of the contents of this book. The information contained in this book is strictly for educational purposes. Therefore, if you wish to apply ideas contained in this book, you are taking full responsibility for your actions.
The author and publisher disclaim any warranties (express or implied), merchantability, for any particular purpose. The author and publisher shall in no event be held liable to any party for any direct, indirect, punitive, special, incidental or other consequential damages arising directly or indirectly from any use of this material, which is provided "as is", and without warranties.

Introduction

Speedy preparation snacks are ideal for individuals and families who are busy and on-the-go. Just include a few additional food items on your shopping list so you have the right ingredients on-hand to prepare your snacks.

These recipes are extremely versatile. Prepare these snacks on the spot or prepare the night before or first thing in the morning. Simply bring them to work or include them with your child's lunch.

I've organized these easy-prep snack recipes into a number of different categories to allow for fast and simple look-up. I have also included a few recipes from my other book titled *Green Smoothie Recipes & other Healthy Smoothie Recipes.*

Whenever possible, I recommend utilizing gluten-free options. Individuals who suffer from Celiac disease can experience extreme symptoms due to their body's intolerance of gluten. However many people are unaware they have gluten sensitivities as their symptoms are often only mild, such as bloating and tiredness, which they often attribute to other causes.

According to some sources, 1 in 33 people suffer from Celiac disease, though some experts claim the real figure is much higher. According to osteopathic physician and author Dr Mercola, as many as 10% of people have some degree of gluten sensitivity or intolerance.

What's more, gluten-free breads and foods tend to be healthier and they allow for easier, more efficient digestion. This makes gluten-free foods more nutritious, so I have included a number of gluten-free snack recipes in this book.

Healthy Snack Preparation

Healthy snacking is key to maintaining a healthy weight. Unfortunately, unhealthy snacks such as chips, candy bars and cookies tend to be easily accessible and there's little, if any, prep required. This makes these less-than-healthy foods more appealing to busy, on-the-go individuals.

These easy-to-prepare recipes are sure to make healthy snacking much easier and more convenient! When your life is busy, there's often a great deal of stress involved too and this can leave you prone to opportunistic illness like colds and flu bugs. But these easy snack recipes will help keep you looking and feeling your best!

Healthy, homemade snacks aren't just for stay-at-home moms or retired folks! These recipes are designed to be viable for you, even if you have a hectic, busy schedule.

These snack recipes are perfect for children. In fact, they're so simple to prepare that your kids can make up many of their own snacks! Adult eating habits are largely influenced by the foods that you eat as a child, so healthy eating is extremely important during childhood!

These recipes will also help encourage creative snacking habits, which can make for a much richer snacking experience. Kids in particular also tend to be attracted to bright colors, so the wide array of fruits and veggies mentioned in this book will help keep snack time appealing! A bit of inventiveness and creativity can go a long way in the kitchen!

In this book, you'll find lots of healthy alternative to the many popular, yet unhealthy foods that are commonly consumed as snacks. Instead of potato chips, opt for some tortilla chips dipped in homemade salsa or dip fruits in yogurt or honey.

Fruit smoothies are also great for snack time. Plus, they're easy to eat on the go! In fact, you don't even need to keep a supply of fresh fruits on-hand. Freeze a bit of fruit or buy frozen berries. Then, simply thaw and blend when it's time for a snack!

Pair your smoothie with some fresh fruits and veggies, dipped in yogurt or hummus.

Salads also make for a very healthy, easy-to-prepare snack. Salads also make a great pack-and-go snack that you can take along to work or school. And you can use whatever you have on-hand, such as lettuce, carrots, cucumbers, even a bit of chicken or cheese. Preparing a pre-made salad at home can be a huge money saver too, as by comparison, salads can be quite expensive when purchased at the local restaurant or supermarket.

Salt Alternatives

I recommend using Himalayan salt in recipes that call for salt as an ingredient.

The body does need salt to remain healthy and balanced, but table salt isn't the right type. Table salt has been chemically processed into sodium chloride. This is different from salt in its natural form and as a result, your body cannot use it properly. It requires a lot of water for your body to process sodium chloride. This results in imbalances that can cause or exacerbate serious health problems. It can also lead to dehydration.

Himalayan salt is pure and it has not been chemically processed, therefore, it maintains its beneficial attributes and components such as minerals. Himalayan salt, when consumed in small amounts, can serve to help promote healthy sleep patterns, cardiovascular health, healthy skin and an overall balance in your body chemistry, pH and fluids.

Individuals who have been diagnosed with ailments such as high blood pressure may need to avoid salt entirely, even Himalayan salt. Fortunately, there are a number of herbal alternatives to salt.

1. Garlic – Garlic is an extremely popular, flavorful seasoning. It's used in many regions of the world, from Europe to the Mediterranean to South America and beyond. It's extremely versatile, as it can be dried, sauteed, roasted or boiled. Garlic is a nice salt substitute or you can use it as a supplement to salt, thereby enabling you to maintain flavor without using quite as much salt.

2. Chives – The tiniest member of the onion family, chives are ideal for use in many dishes in place of salt. Chives are suitable for use in dishes with potato, salads or seafood recipes.

3. Basil – Basil is commonplace in many Italian dishes. It's also found in some forms of Asian cuisine. Basil is a great herb, which can be added to vegetable dishes either in its dried or fresh form.

4. Oregano – Oregano is most often found in Mediterranean, Middle Eastern and Spanish-Latin cuisine. It's frequently combined with basil for use on grilled poultry and vegetable dishes. Like basil, oregano is an herb that can be used dry or fresh.

5. Sage – Sage isn't just for your stuffing dishes! It's ideal for Italian recipes, meat and even soups.

6. Ginger – Well-known for its ability to soothe your digestive system, this strong, distinctive herb is commonly used in Asian recipes. It's suitable for use in meat dishes, veggies and soup.

No-Prep Snack Ideas

1. Nuts – Almonds and pistachios make for a great, very portable snack. A handful of nuts averages approximately 100 calories and they tend to be very filling too. High in protein and fiber, your blood sugar will remain constant too.

2. Hard-boiled eggs – High in protein, low in calories and fat, hard-boiled eggs are a great snack that stores well. They're also a great on-the-go breakfast item that's easy to make more appealing to children with a quick and simple egg dying project!

    Another alternative: raw egg from a fresh, organic free-range hen. Dip a bit of bread in the raw egg or soft-boil and leave the yolk uncooked and runny.

3. Hummus – High in fiber and protein, Hummus is a dip made of chick peas and sesame paste or tahini. Eat it with a bit of pita bread or crackers. 2 teaspoons of on bread or crackers averages 100 calories.

    For a gluten-free option, plus a serving of veggies, pair the hummus with vegetables such as celery or carrots.

4. Chocolate – If you're craving chocolate, try a bit of dark chocolate. Opt for a chocolate with a high cocoa percentage such as 70, 80 or 90%. The higher the percentage, the richer it tastes, and there's less sugar. Though be warned that high cocoa percentages can taste slightly bitter. Cocoa is high in antioxidants, but eat it in moderation!

5. Blueberries – A cup of blueberries has just 75 calories and like chocolate, they have lots of antioxidants. Antioxidants

protect your body's cells from free radicals and they can even reduce your risk of stroke and neuro-degenerative diseases.

6. Bananas – Bananas are high in potassium and a medium one packs just 100 calories. You can even pair banana slices with cheese slices or dip in yogurt.

7. Watermelon – Watermelons are very filling and low in calories, with only 100 in a medium watermelon! The high water content will help keep you hydrated too!

Gluten-Free Bread Recipes for Healthy Snacking

Tips

When it's time to make up a sandwich, consider a healthy, gluten-free alternative. There are many gluten-free products such as flax seed or bean crackers and breads that are widely available at most grocery stores and health food supermarkets.

This section will provide recipes for four different bread recipes, all gluten-free and Celiac-friendly. You can eat these breads as a snack with bit of honey, cheese or jam, or use a couple slices for your next sandwich.

In addition, these recipes freeze well, so it's possible to double or triple the recipe, then simply freeze the loaves for future use.

A number of the recipes in this book are gluten-free (GF) or you can make a gluten-free variation by substituting an ingredient or two.

Rice Flour Sandwich Bread

Recipe Ingredients:

2 1/4 teaspoons of Xanthan gum

2 1/4 teaspoons of active dry yeast

3 tablespoons of vegetable oil

3 1/2 tablespoons of granulated sugar

1/2 cup of powdered milk

1 1/2 cups of brown rice flour

1 1/2 cups of water

2 cups of white rice flour

3 extra large eggs (beaten)

Cooking Directions:

Place all of the dry ingredients in a large mixing bowl and blend.

Combine the wet ingredients in a mixing bowl and blend thoroughly.

Combine the dry and wet ingredients and blend until the dough batter has a thick consistency.

Place the dough in a greased loaf pan and cover it with a clean cloth.

Place the dough in a warm location and allow the dough to rise for 1 hour.

Preheat your oven to a temperature of 375 degrees.

Bake the dough for 50 to 60 minutes. The top and edges should be golden brown in colour.

Serving Instructions, Variations and Tips:

Yield: 1 loaf, approximately 12 slices.

If desired, substitute the vegetable oil with sunflower oil.

Optional ingredient: Add 1 1/2 teaspoons of salt.

Free Bread

Recipe Ingredients:
¼ of a banana (mashed)

½ a lemon

½ teaspoon of bicarbonate of soda

2 cups of tapioca flour

3 cups of chickpea flour

4 cups of water

Cooking Directions:
Soak the chickpea flour in 3 cups of water for approximately 2 hours.

Preheat your oven to 350 degrees Fahrenheit.

Combine the flours and the remaining 1 cup of water.

Mix well until it reaches a thick batter consistency.

Add the banana and blend.

Juice the lemon and stir in the lemon juice.

Add the bicarbonate of soda and mix thoroughly.

Pour the bread batter into to a greased bread tin.

Bake for approximately 45 to 60 minutes.

Serving Instructions, Variations and Tips:
This recipe is free of eggs, yeast, gluten and sugar.

Bananas are used in place of eggs in this recipe.

Alternatively, try apple sauce.

If desired, experiment with different flours and ingredients.

If desired, use 1 cup of tapioca flour and 1 cup of brown rice flour in place of the tapioca flour.

You can substitute the chickpea flour with brown rice flour or another variety.

Simple and Sweet Apple Bread

Recipe Ingredients:

1/4 teaspoon of salt

1/2 teaspoon of baking soda

3/4 teaspoon of ground cinnamon

1 teaspoon of gluten-free baking powder

1 teaspoon apple cider vinegar

2 teaspoons of xanthum gum

1/3 cup of whole bean flour

1/3 cup of cornstarch

1/2 cup of granulated sugar

1 cup of raisins

1 1/3 cup of sorghum flour

1 1/2 cup of chunky apple sauce

2 egg whites (beaten)

Cooking Directions:

Preheat your oven to 350 degrees Fahrenheit.

Grease and flour a large bread pan.

Pour the dry ingredients into a large mixing bowl and blend them thoroughly.

Place the vinegar, apple sauce and egg whites in a bowl and mix well.

Stir in the vinegar, egg whites and apple sauce into the dry ingredients.

Pour the batter into the greased-and-floured baking pan.

Bake for approximately 55 to 60 minutes.

Serving Instructions, Variations and Tips:

Yield: 1 loaf.

Allow the bread to cool before serving.

Homemade Banana Bread

Recipe Ingredients:

1 1/4 teaspoon of vanilla extract

2 teaspoons of baking powder

2 cups of rice flour

1 full stick of butter

2 large eggs

3 1/2 large bananas (ripe and mashed)

Cooking Directions:

Allow the butter to soften at room temperature.

Preheat the oven to 325.

Grease and flour a 9-inch bread pan.

Use a mixer to blend the sugar and butter into a creamy consistency.

Combine the sugar and butter with the eggs, bananas and vanilla.

Mix the dry ingredients in a large mixing bowl.

Gradually blend the wet and dry ingredients to form the batter.

Pour the batter into the bread pan.

Bake for approximately 70 to 80 minutes. The crust should be golden brown.

Serving Instructions, Variations and Tips:

Yield: 1 loaf.

Optional ingredient: 1 cup of granulated sugar.

If desired, add 1 cup of chopped nuts (such as almonds) to the batter.

Use gluten-free vanilla extract for this recipe.

Healthy Snacks for Adults

Pasta Snacks

Pasta With Sun-dried Tomatoes

Recipe Ingredients:

1 Box of pasta

Jar of sun-dried tomatoes

Olive oil

Black pepper

Salt

Cooking Directions:

Boil the pasta for 10-15 minutes depending on the variety. The pasta should be soft and tender, not mushy or rubbery.

Drain the water from the pasta.

Stir in the sun-dried tomatoes.

Pour in a dash of olive oil. Mix well.

Top with a dash of salt and freshly-ground black pepper.

Serving Instructions, Variations and Tips:

Optional ingredient: Grated cheese can be sprinkled over the top of this dish immediately before serving.

A few great pasta varieties for this recipe include whole wheat pasta, spelt or a gluten-free variety such as rice pasta or corn and millet pasta.

Cooking tip: Always allow the water to boil before you add the pasta. This prevents the pasta from getting soft and mushy. The saucepan can remain uncovered during the cooking process.

Noodle pasta varieties tend to cook very quickly, so monitor closely. When finished, the pasta should be soft and tender but not mushy.

Speedy Pesto Pasta Dish

Recipe Ingredients:

1 Box of pasta

Pesto sauce

Cooking Directions:

Boil the pasta for 10-15 minutes depending on pasta type.

Drain away the water from the pasta.

Stir in the the pesto sauce.

Serving Instructions, Variations and Tips:

Optional ingredient: Sliced mushrooms can be stirred into the pasta right after it's finished cooking.

Optional ingredient: Grated garlic can be added and stirred into the pasta right before serving.

Remember that many pasta sauces include garlic, so you may want to skip this ingredient if you are using a sauce with garlic.

Creamy Oregano and Olive Pasta

Recipe Ingredients:

1 Box of pasta

Sliced olives

Double cream

Oregano

Grated cheese

Cooking Directions:

Boil the pasta for approximately 10 to 15 minutes. The precise cooking time will vary according to pasta variety. It must be soft and tender.

Drain away the water.

Stir in the oregano, olives and cream. Blend well.

Sprinkle grated cheese over top of the pasta immediately before serving.

Serving Instructions, Variations and Tips:

For a healthier snack, opt for organic cream for this recipe.

Any variety of pasta will work for this recipe.

Make a gluten-free variation of this dish by using wheat-free pasta or another gluten-free variety of pasta.

This simple pasta dish is quite filling and it's appealing to most children, though some kids may prefer an olive-free version.

Tuna Pasta

Recipe Ingredients:

1 Box of pasta

1 Can of tuna

Fresh basil (chopped)

Grated cheese

Olive oil

Cooking Directions:

Boil the pasta for approximately 10 to 15 minutes. The pasta must be soft and tender.

Drain the water from the pasta

Mix in the basil, tuna and olive oil.

Sprinkle grated cheese on top or provide the cheese as a side when serving.

Serving Instructions, Variations and Tips:

Add a bit of olive oil to this or any other pasta dish. The pasta with olive oil can make for a great snack when eaten alone.

Optional ingredients: If desired, add salt and pepper to taste.

Any variety of pasta will work for this recipe.

Make a gluten-free variation of this dish by using wheat-free pasta or another gluten-free variety of pasta.

Lentil Soup Over Pasta

Recipe Ingredients:

1 Box of pasta

Fresh basil (chopped)

Fresh parsley (chopped)

1 Can of lentil soup

Cooking Directions:

Boil the pasta for approximately 10 to 15 minutes. The pasta must be soft and tender.

Drain the water from the pasta.

Pour the lentil soup into a saucepan and heat it.

Combine the pasta and the soup in a large bowl.

Sprinkle in the chopped parsley and basil.

Serving Instructions, Variations and Tips:

Optional ingredients: If desired, add salt and pepper to taste.

Make a gluten-free variation of this dish by using wheat-free pasta or another gluten-free variety of pasta.

Vegetable Snacks

Tomato, Onion and Pepper Tortilla Triangles

Recipe Ingredients:

¼ cup of onion (chopped)

1/2 cup of tomato (chopped)

1/2 cup of green pepper (chopped)

1 cup of cheddar cheese (shredded)

4 8-inch soft tortillas

Cooking Directions:

Place the tortilla on a flat surface and sprinkle cheese over it.

Place chunks of chopped onions, green pepper and tomatoes over the cheese.

Fold the tortillas closed to form a half-circle.

Cook each tortilla for 2 minutes in a skillet over medium-high heat.

Flip the tortilla and cook for 1 additional minute.

Serving Instructions, Variations and Tips:

Cut each tortilla into 4 triangles.

Serve with a salsa dip or sour cream.

Ranch Carrot and Cuke Pouches

Recipe Ingredients:

3 tablespoons of creamy ranch dressing

1 carrot (thinly sliced)

1 small cucumber (thinly sliced)

2 pieces of pita bread

Cooking Directions:

Warm the pita bread for a couple minutes in the oven.

Slice the pita bread in half, leaving two half-circles.

Spread ranch dressing onto each side of the pita bread interior.

Place cucumber and carrot slices inside the pita pockets. Serve!

Barbecue Ranch Veggie Sandwiches

Recipe Ingredients:

1 tablespoons of barbecue sauce

3 tablespoons of ranch salad dressing

2 large bun rolls

2 green pepper rings

2 slices of tomato

4 lettuce leaves

4 slices of cucumber

Cooking Directions:

Place the salad dressing and barbecue sauce in a mixing bowl and blend well.

Cut each bun in half.

Apply the barbecue sauce and ranch dressing mix onto each bun half.

Place 2 lettuce leaves on each bun bottom.

Add a tomato slice, a piece of pepper and 2 cucumber slices on top of the lettuce.

Place the bun top on each sandwich and serve.

Serving Instructions, Variations and Tips:

Opt for a salad dressing and barbecue sauce that's sugar-free and natural.

This dish makes a great after-school snack. Simply cut them into small bite-sized pieces.

Pepper and Carrot Tortilla Rolls

Recipe Ingredients:

2 tablespoons of cream cheese

1 carrot (grated)

1 sweet red pepper (finely chopped)

2 soft flour tortillas

Cooking Directions:

Warm the tortillas in the oven.

Place each tortilla on a flat surface and coat each one with a thin layer of cream cheese.

Sprinkle chunks of grated carrot and chopped pepper over the cream cheese.

Roll up the tortillas and serve.

Serving Instructions, Variations and Tips:

Optional ingredients: Fresh spinach can be included in the rolls.

If desired, opt for gluten-free tortillas or a gluten-free bread variety.

Substitute the cream cheese with cottage cheese for a slightly different flavor.

Homemade Sweet Potato Chips

Recipe Ingredients:

1 large sweet potato

Olive oil

Cooking Directions:

Preheat your oven to 350 degrees F.

Slice your sweet potato and place the slices on a baking sheet.

Drizzle olive oil over the potato slices.

Bake the potatoes for 10 minutes.
Remove the baking sheet from the oven and use a spatula to flip the chips.

Bake for an additional 2 minutes. The homemade chips will be golden brown in color when they're done.

Serving Instructions, Variations and Tips:

Optional ingredients: If desired, add salt to taste immediately after adding the olive oil.

Make your chips a bit sweeter by sprinkling cinnamon over the chips just prior to baking.

Homemade Creamy Veggie Pizza

Recipe Ingredients:

¼ teaspoon of salt

½ teaspoon of oregano

½ teaspoon of basil

¾ teaspoon of baking powder

¼ cup of fat free margarine

¼ cup of cream cheese

½ cup of broccoli (chopped)

½ cup of tomato (chopped)

½ cup of red and green bell peppers

½ cup of carrots (shredded)

½ cup of cauliflower (chopped)

1 1/3 cup of flour

1 ½ cup of sour cream

2 egg whites

Cooking Directions:

Allow the cream cheese to soften at room temperature.

Preheat your oven to 400 degrees F.

Separate the egg whites and place them in a large mixing bowl.

Add in the salt, flour, margarine and baking powder.

Hand mix the ingredients and blend well into a dough

consistency.

Apply a non-stick cooking spray to a pizza pan.

Roll out the dough and place it in the pizza pan.

Bake the dough for approximately 10 minutes. It must develop a light golden brown color.

Allow the pizza crust to cool.

Combine basil, oregano, cream cheese and sour cream in a bowl. Mix well.

Spread this mix over the crust in an even layer.

Add the veggies over the entire pizza, right up to the edges.

Serving Instructions, Variations and Tips:

This recipe works well with traditional plain white flour or gluten-free plain flour varieties.

Pumpkin Cream Cheese Crackers

Recipe Ingredients:

1 teaspoon of cinnamon

¼ can of pecans (finely chopped)

1 4-ounce package of cream cheese

1 15-ounce can of pureed pumpkin

Graham crackers

Cooking Directions:

Place the pumpkin in a small saucepan.

Warm the pumpkin over low heat. Stir to ensure even warming, then remove from heat.

Stir in the pecans and cinnamon. Blend well.

Allow mixture to cool for approximately 3 to 5 minutes.

Mix in the cream cheese and blend evenly.

Spread over crackers and serve.

Serving Instructions, Variations and Tips:

Optional ingredients: If desired, use pears, strawberries or apple slices in this dish as a substitute for pumpkin.

This recipe can serve as a delicious fresh fruit dip.

If desired, use a different cracker type in place of graham crackers.

This recipe makes a great appetizer or after-school snack.

Quick and Simple Celery Boats

Recipe Ingredients:

½ cup of granola

2 stalks of celery

Cream cheese

Raisins

Cooking Directions:

Allow the cream cheese to soften at room temperature.

Rinse each celery stalk and cut them into 5 or 6 pieces.

Spread cream cheese over the celery segments.

Spread the celery pieces with the cream cheese.

Sprinkle granola over the cream cheese.

Sprinkle raisins over the celery boats.

Serving Instructions, Variations and Tips:

If desired, substitute the cream cheese with a cheese spread or peanut butter.

Press the granola into the cheese to prevent it from falling off.

This works well as an appetizer or a healthy after school snack for the kids!

Baked Carrot Chunks

Recipe Ingredients:

12 carrots

Olive oil

Himalayan salt

Cooking Directions:

Preheat your oven to 375 degrees F.

Trim and rinse the carrots.

Cut each carrot in half (or quarters if you have large carrots.)

Place the cut carrots in a mixing bowl.

Pour a few teaspoons of olive oil into the bowl and thoroughly coat the carrots.

Lay the carrots on a baking sheet in a single layer.

Sprinkle Himalayan salt over the oil-covered carrots.

Bake for approximately 25 minutes. When finished, the carrots will take on a light brown tone.

Serving Instructions, Variations and Tips:

If desired, substitute the salt with cinnamon.

These carrots go well with a dip – perfect for an appetizer dish.

Roasted Cauliflower Chunks

Recipe Ingredients:

¼ teaspoon of chili powder

1 cup of seasoned bread crumbs

1 head of cauliflower

2 garlic cloves (finely minced)

Olive oil

Cooking Directions:

Preheat your oven to 400 degrees F.

Trim and rinse the cauliflower. Cut it into bite-sized chunks.

Spoon a few tablespoons of olive oil into a large mixing bowl.

Place the cauliflower florets in the oil and coat thoroughly.

Place the oil-coated cauliflower chunks on a baking sheet.

Slide the baking sheet in to the preheated oven and roast for 15 minutes.

Place the bread crumbs in a mixing bowl and coat with olive oil.

Combine the bread crumbs with chili powder and garlic. Toss to thoroughly mix.

Remove the cauliflower chunks from the oven after 15 minutes and flip.

Sprinkle the breadcrumb mix over the cauliflower.

Place the baking sheet in the oven and roast for an

additional 10 minutes. The cauliflower will be golden and tender; the breadcrumbs will be lightly toasted.

Serving Instructions, Variations and Tips:

Serve immediately after you finish roasting. If you wait too long to serve, the cauliflower may get a rather soft and mushy.

Experiment with different seasonings on this dish.

Asparagus on Cream Cheese and Crackers

Recipe Ingredients:

1 teaspoon of lemon juice

1 tablespoon of water

2.5 ounces of Parmesan and Romano cheese (shredded)

2 3-ounce packages of cream cheese

12 asparagus spears

Assorted crackers

Cooking Directions:

Allow the cream cheese to soften at room temperature.

Trim and wash the asparagus spears.

Cut the asparagus into bite-sized pieces.

Fill a pan with water and bring to a boil.

Stream the asparagus until it's soft and tender.

Pour out excess water.

Combine the cream cheese, lemon juice and shredded Parmesan and Romano cheese in a mixing bowl.

Blend well and spread over your crackers.

Top each cracker with a chunk of asparagus.

Serving Instructions, Variations and Tips:

If desired, use chive-flavored cream cheese or a veggie cream cheese variety in place of the homemade topping.

Crème Fraiche and Butternut Over Bread

Recipe Ingredients:

1 tablespoon of butter

2 tablespoons of crème fraiche

Bread

Butternut squash (diced)

Mushrooms (chopped)

Chives (chopped)

Salt and pepper

Cooking Directions:

Place a large skillet over medium-high heat.

Place the butter, pepper and salt in the skillet.

Add the butternut squash and fry until the squash is tender and soft.

Mash the squash with a large fork and remove from heat.

Fry the mushrooms in butter over medium-high heat.

Fry in butter the mushrooms.

Place the crème fraiche in a bowl and mix in the chives. Blend well.

Toast a few pieces of bread.

Spread the crème fraiche over the bread.

Spread the squash over the crème fraiche.

Top with mushrooms and serve.

Simple and Speedy Rice Florentine

Recipe Ingredients:

1/4 teaspoon of ground white pepper

1/4 teaspoon of dried whole rosemary (crushed)

1 tablespoon of butter or margarine

1/3 cup of pine nuts (toasted)

1/2 cup sliced green onions

1/2 cup of freshly-grated Parmesan cheese

3 cups of cooked rice

1/2 pound of fresh spinach

1 medium red bell pepper (chopped)

3 cloves of garlic (minced)

Cooking Directions:

Remove the spinach stems.

Wash the leaves and divide the leaves into large chunks.

Melt 1 tablespoon of butter in large skillet over medium-high heat.

Add the red peppers, spinach, garlic, onions, rosemary and pepper to the skillet.

Cook for approximately 2 to 3 minutes. The spinach must be soft.

Add the cooked rice, nuts and cheese.

Blend and stir the ingredients in the skillet over medium

heat. The contents must be well-heated and the cheese must melt.

Serving Instructions, Variations and Tips:

Serve immediately.

Bean Snacks

Speedy-Prep Bean Stew

Recipe Ingredients:

1 can of hominy (canned)

1 can of kidney beans

1 can of pinto beans

1 can of garbanzo beans

6-ounces of tomato sauce

1 packet of taco seasoning

Cooking Directions:

Mix the beans in a large bowl.

Add the tomato sauce and taco seasoning and blend well.

Heat and serve.

Serving Instructions, Variations and Tips:

This recipe makes approximately 6 servings.

Whenever possible, opt for a sugar-free tomato sauce variety.

Speedy Spicy Beans and Lentils

Recipe Ingredients:

1 can of lentils

1 can of pinto beans

1 can of garbanzo beans

1 can of kidney beans

1 can of great northern whites

1 can of French onion soup

Salad dressing

Barbecue sauce

Cooking Directions:

Combine the lentils and beans in a large saucepan.

Add the soup to the lentils and beans.

Warm the ingredients over medium-low heat until it's thoroughly warmed.

Serving Instructions, Variations and Tips:

Serve hot.

Add the dressing and sauce according to taste.

Opt for a low-fat dressing and barbecue sauce.

Black Bean Nachos

Recipe Ingredients:

1 can of black beans (drained)

1 bag of tortilla chips

1 tomato (chopped)

1 onion (chopped)

Shredded cheese

Cooking Directions:

Preheat your oven to 300 degrees F.

Spread the chips over a serving dish.

Place a spoonful of beans onto each chip.

Add a bit of tomato and onion to each chip.

Sprinkle with shredded cheese.

Bake for approximately 3 minutes or until the cheese has melted.

Serving Instructions, Variations and Tips:

Serve warm.

This recipe makes for a great appetizer or party platter.

Baked Chickpeas

Recipe Ingredients:

1 tin of cooked chickpeas

Olive oil

Salt

Cooking Directions:

Preheat your oven to 400 degrees F.

Drain the chickpeas and remove the skins.

Pour the chickpeas onto a paper towel and use another paper towel to pat dry.

Place the chickpeas in a bowl and coat them with the oil.

Distribute the chickpeas on a cookie sheet.

Add a dash of salt.

Bake for approximately 30 minutes. They will be crunchy and slightly browned.

Serving Instructions, Variations and Tips:

Store in an air-tight container.

If desired, use coconut oil in place of olive oil.

Kidney beans can also be integrated into this recipe.

If desired, add seasoning after they're removed from the oven. Popular seasonings include cayenne pepper, garlic powder, curry and cumin.

Quick-Prep Bean and Rice Burritos

Recipe Ingredients:

1/4 can of cooked beans

1/4 can or packet of cooked rice

1 tortilla

Pesto or salsa

Lettuce (shredded)

Monterey Jack cheese

Cooking Directions:

Preheat your oven to 350 degrees F.

Pour the rice and beans into a bowl and mix.

Spoon the rice and bean mix onto the tortillas.

Add the pesto or salsa on top of the beans.

Roll up the tortillas and place on a baking sheet. Cook for approximately 10 minutes.

Unwrap the tortillas and add the cheese and lettuce. Roll closed and serve.

Serving Instructions, Variations and Tips:

You can use other cheese varieties for this dish. Opt for a low-fat variety whenever possible.

Use gluten-free tortillas to make this dish Celiac-friendly.

If you don't like crispy tortillas, bake them in aluminum foil.

Fruit Snacks

Cheese and Apple Toast

Recipe Ingredients:

1 1/2 cup apple sauce

4 slices of toast

4 slice of cheese

Nutmeg

Cooking Directions:

Stir a bit of nutmeg into the apple sauce.

Spread a few spoons of apple sauce onto each piece of toast.

Place a slice of cheese over the apple sauce.

Bake the toast over medium heat for a couple minutes. The cheese must melt.

Serving Instructions, Variations and Tips:

Serve hot.

This recipe serves 4 people.

Whenever possible, use homemade sugar-free apple sauce.

Cheese and Fruit Kebabs

Recipe Ingredients:

1 cup of grapes

1 cup of kiwi (cubed)

1 cup of apples (cubed)

1 cup of strawberries (quartered)

1-pound block of cheddar cheese (cubed)

4 skewers

Cooking Directions:

Alternate between cheese, kiwi, apple, cheese, strawberry, and grape onto each skewer.

Serving Instructions, Variations and Tips:

If desired, alternate between one fruit type and cheese on each skewer.

An array of other fruits and berries will work for this snack!

Banana Blackberry Milkshake

Recipe Ingredients:

¼ pint of fresh blackberries

1 pint of milk

1 banana (chopped)

6 ice cubes

Sugar substitute

Vanilla essence

Cooking Directions:

Pour the milk into a food processor or blender.

Add the ice cubes, bananas and blackberries.

Blend until the mixture is smooth and well-blended.

Add the sugar substitute and blend momentarily to mix.

Serving Instructions, Variations and Tips:

Serve immediately.

Use organic raw milk whenever possible.

Popular sugar substitutes include xylitol, stevia and honey. Remember that xylitol is very toxic to cats and dogs, so don't share with your pets if you use this ingredient!

Cheesey Pineapple Tortilla

Recipe Ingredients:

1 8-ounce container of cream cheese

1 11-ounce can of sliced pineapple (in juice)

6 soft tortilla wraps

Whipped cream

Cooking Directions:

Spread cream cheese over the tortillas.

Slice a pineapple ring in half and place the halves on the tortilla.

Spoon a bit of whipped cream over the pineapple.

Roll each tortilla and serve.

Serving Instructions, Variations and Tips:

This recipe makes 6 servings.

If desired, use Greek yogurt in place of whipped topping.

Fruit and Oat Snack Bars

Recipe Ingredients:

1 teaspoon of baking soda

1 teaspoon of cinnamon

2 teaspoon of vanilla extract

2 tablespoons of oil

2 tablespoons of milk

1 cup of brown sugar

1 cup of dried mixed fruit

1 1/2 cup of all purpose flour

3 cups of quick oats (uncooked)

1 8-ounce container of vanilla yogurt

2 egg whites (lightly beaten)

Cooking Directions:

Preheat your oven to 350 degrees F.

Place the sugar in a bowl, along with the egg whites and yogurt.

Stir in the vanilla, oil and milk. Blend well.

Combine the cinnamon, flour and baking soda in a medium bowl.

Combine the contents of the two bowls and mix well with a spatula.

Stir in the oats and dried fruit.

Spoon the mixture into an ungreased baking pan and compress with a spatula.

Bake for approximately 25 minutes. The bars must take on a light brown color.

Serving Instructions, Variations and Tips:

This recipe makes 10 servings.

Allow the bars to cool, then cut into squares.

Dried fruits are full of nutrients and this recipe makes a perfect snack for anyone on the go. It's also a great morning snack.

For a healthier variation, use a natural sugar substitute.

Homemade Polynesian Bars

Recipe Ingredients:

1/2 teaspoon of salt

1/2 cup of nuts (chopped)

1/2 cup of unsweetened coconut

3/4 cup of margarine

1 1/2 cups of flour

1 1/2 cups of rolled oats

Filling:

1 teaspoon of vanilla

1/4 cup water

4 cups of dates (chopped)

1 to 2 cans of crushed pineapple

Cooking Directions:

Mix the ingredients for the filling and heat until it's smooth and thick in consistency.

Preheat your oven to 350 degrees F.

Add the dry ingredients to a large bowl and mix well.

Grease a medium baking pan.

Pour half of the crumb mix into the pan and press it down with a spatula.

Add the filling and spread it over the layer of crumb mix.

Apply the rest of the dry ingredient mix over the filling and compress with a spatula.

Bake for approximately 30 minutes. They should be golden brown in colour.

Serving Instructions, Variations and Tips:

Allow the bars to cool, then cut them into snack-sized squares.

For a low-calorie variation of this recipe, substitute the margarine with 1 cup of orange juice.

For a Celiac-friendly recipe, use gluten-free or millet flour.

If desired, experiment with different nuts and fruits in this snack recipe. Some prefer dried apricots in place of dates.

Banana and Peanut Butter Burritos

Recipe Ingredients:

4 tablespoons of plain yogurt

4 tablespoons of peanut butter (creamy variety)

2 bananas (thinly sliced)

4 6-inch flour tortillas

Cooking Directions:

Spread peanut butter over each tortilla. Leave a 1-inch peanut butter-free border around the perimeter.

Lay banana slices over the peanut butter.

Spread a thin layer of yogurt over the bananas.

Fold the tortilla and roll it closed.

Serving Instructions, Variations and Tips:

This recipe makes 4 servings.

If desired, use vanilla yogurt in place of plain. You can also use an array of different fruits for this recipe.

Try this recipe without the yogurt, if desired.

Homemade Granola Snack

Recipe Ingredients:

½ teaspoon of cinnamon

1 teaspoon of vanilla

¼ cup of vegetable oil

1/3 cup of honey

3 cups of of rolled oats

Your choice of nuts, seeds and dried fruit

Cooking Directions:

Preheat your oven to 300 degrees F.

Combine and blend the salt, oats and cinnamon.

Pour the oil, vanilla and honey into a small bowl and mix well.

Pour the wet ingredients into the oat mix and blend very thoroughly so the oats are totally coated.

Spread a thin layer of the granola mix over a cookie sheet.

Place the cookie sheet on the center oven shelf and bake for 15 minutes.

Open the oven and stir the granola.

Bake for an additional 5 to 15 minutes. The granola must take on pale golden brown color.

Stir the granola as it cools to prevent it from clumping.

Add in other ingredients such as nuts, seeds and dried fruit.

Serving Instructions, Variations and Tips:

This snack goes well with fresh raw milk or coconut milk.

If desired, add rolled grain flakes to this recipe.

If desired, add a dash of salt to this recipe.

Store your homemade granola in an air-tight container and eat it within 2 weeks.

For a crunchier granola, bake for a few additional minutes.

Berry Yogurt Crunch

Recipe Ingredients:

3 tablespoons of granola

3 tablespoons of plain yogurt

Fresh berries

Cooking Directions:

Place the yogurt in a large parfait cup.

Add the granola to the yogurt and mix.

Sprinkle fresh berries over the granola and yogurt, then serve.

Serving Instructions, Variations and Tips:

This protein-packed snack is ideal for on-the-go individuals.

If desired, substitute fresh banana, kiwi, apple slices or other fruit in place of the berries.

Speedy Blueberry Yogurt Shake

Recipe Ingredients:

2 cups of blueberries

2 cups of plain yogurt

Cooking Directions:

Place the yogurt in a blender or food processor.

Add the blueberries.

Blend the ingredients until they reach a smoothie/milkshake consistency.

Serving Instructions, Variations and Tips:

This recipe makes 2 servings.

This is a great night time snack for the kids.

Use thick straws to drink this shake.

Popcorn and Dried Fruit

Recipe Ingredients:

1 cup of dried banana chips

1 cup of nuts or seeds

1 cup of dried cranberries

2 cups of popcorn

Cooking Directions:

Place the dried cranberries and bananas into a Tupperware container.

Add the nuts, seeds and popcorn.

Close tightly and shake until mixed thoroughly together.

Serving Instructions, Variations and Tips:

This recipe makes 4 servings.

If desired, substitute different dried fruit varieties.

Store in an air-tight Tupperware container.

Sandwich Snacks

Apple Cinnamon Sandwiches

Recipe Ingredients:

1 tablespoons of butter

1 tablespoon of cinnamon

4 slices of apple bread

1 apple (peeled, core removed and sliced)

Cooking Directions:

Preheat your oven temperature on the grill or broil setting.

Spread butter over the bread slices and lay the on an ungreased baking sheet.

Add a few apple slices to the buttered bread.

Sprinkle a bit of cinnamon over the apples.

Broil or grill for approximately 2 minutes. They should be a pale golden brown color.

Serving Instructions, Variations and Tips:

This recipe makes 4 servings.

Consult the gluten-free bread section for the apple bread recipe!

Chicken Apple Sandwiches

Recipe Ingredients:

1 teaspoon of fresh ginger-root (grated)

2 1/4 teaspoons of lemon juice

1/2 cup of mayonnaise

1 cup of cooked chicken

1 bunch of watercress

1 Braeburn apple

1 celery rib (chopped)

1 medium red onion (peeled and thinly sliced)

1 baguette

Cooking Directions:

Cut the chicken into bite-sized pieces.

Chop the Braeburn apple into small, bite-sized chunks.

Combine the lemon juice, ginger and mayonnaise in a mixing bowl.

Add the celery, apple and chicken. Mix well.

Slice the baguette.

Place watercress on one side of the baguette and place the mix on the other side.

Place an onion on top and serve.

Serving Instructions, Variations and Tips:

This recipe makes 4 servings.

If desired, use basil or another herb in place of watercress.

Season to taste with salt and pepper.

Speedy-Prep Egg Salad Sandwiches

Recipe Ingredients:

1/4 teaspoon of ground black pepper

1/2 teaspoon of salt

1/2 cup of mayonnaise

6 large eggs

8 slices of bread

Cooking Directions:

Make hard-boiled eggs by boiling them for approximately 10 minutes.

Place the eggs in a bowl of ice water and allow them to cool.

Remove the eggshells.

Slice the eggs in half and place them in a bowl. Mash the eggs with a fork.

Add the mayo, pepper and salt.

Spread the egg salad onto on bread and serve.

Serving Instructions, Variations and Tips:

This recipe will make 4 servings.

If desired, make a gluten-free variation of this dish by using gluten-free bread.

Some enjoy dried onion flakes for added flavor.

Zucchini and Chutney Turkey Salad Sandwich

Recipe Ingredients:

1 teaspoon of sesame seeds (toasted)

2 tablespoons of olive oil

2 tablespoons of Caesar dressing

3 tablespoons of mayonnaise

4 teaspoons of Dijon mustard

1/3 cup of hot mango chutney

1/2 cup of celery (finely chopped)

2 cups of cooked turkey (chopped into small pieces)

7-ounces of roasted red bell peppers (drained and sliced)

1 zucchini

8 spinach leaves

Cooking Directions:

Preheat your oven to 350 degrees F.

Cut the zucchini lengthwise into 1/4-inch wide slices.

Place the turkey, mayonnaise, chutney, celery and sesame seeds in medium bowl and mix. Thoroughly coat the meat.

Brush a bit of olive oil onto each piece of bread.

Lay the bread (in 1 layer) onto a cookie sheet.

Bake for approximately 12 minutes. The bread must be golden and lightly toasted.

Apply a bit of turkey salad to 4 pieces of bread.

Stack the peppers, spinach leaves and zucchini on top of the turkey salad.

Drip a bit of salad dressing over the veggies.

Apply some mustard to the other 4 pieces of bread and top the veggies to complete the sandwiches.

Serving Instructions, Variations and Tips:

If desired, use ranch dressing or another favorite dressing variety. You can also use different veggies.

Veggie Chicken Salad

Recipe Ingredients:

3/4 teaspoon of dry mustard

1/2 teaspoon of seasoned salt

1/2 teaspoon of freshly ground pepper

3 tablespoons of lemon juice

1/3 cup mayonnaise

1/2 cup of green bell peppers (chopped)

1/2 cup of onions (chopped)

1 cup of fresh bean sprouts

1 cup of celery (chopped)

3 cups of cooked chicken breast (chopped)

Cooking Directions:

In a large bowl, combine the sprouts, green peppers, onion, chicken, sprouts and celery.

Blend the remaining ingredients in a bowl.

Mix the contents of the 2 bowls and gently toss to combine.

Serving Instructions, Variations and Tips:

This recipe serves 8 people.

Cheese, Spinach and Pastrami Sandwich

Recipe Ingredients:

1/2 teaspoon of black pepper

1 teaspoon of crushed dried red pepper flakes

2 1/2 cups of baby spinach salad

4 ounces of Caraway Havarti cheese (sliced)

8 ounces of Brie (remove the rind)

8 ounces aged Swiss cheese (sliced)

8 ounces of pastrami (sliced)

1 stick of unsalted butter

1 medium red onion (sliced)

Bread

Cooking Directions:

Set out the butter and allow it to soften at room temperature.

Toast 3 slices of bread

Place the Brie, spices and butter in a food processor and mix.

Spread the Brie on 12 of the bread slices. Apply it to both sides of 6 pieces.

Stack the pastrami, Swiss, spinach and onions.

Add the bread that's coated on both sides.

Stack the rest of the onions, spinach and Havarti.

Top with another slice of bread.

Serving Instructions, Variations and Tips:

This recipe serves 6.

Serve with Dijon mustard if desired.

Plain Brie or a variety with herbs will work for this recipe.

Meat, Cheese and Veggie Sandwiches

Recipe Ingredients:
Spread
1/4 cup of mayonnaise

1 tablespoon of prepared mustard

Sandwich
2 red onion (sliced and divided into rings)

2 tomatoes (sliced)

4 lettuce leaves

8 slices of bread

12 slices of meat

14 large slices cheese

Cooking Directions:
Mix the mustard and mayonnaise in a bowl.

Diagonally slice 6 pieces of cheese.

Spread the mayo and mustard combo onto the bread.

Top 4 pieces of bread with the meat, veggies and cheese.

Top with another piece of bread.

Serving Instructions, Variations and Tips:
This recipe makes 4 sandwiches.

Whole grain bread works well for this recipe.

Caesar Chicken Sandwich

Recipe Ingredients:

1/4 cup of Parmesan cheese (grated)

1/2 cup of creamy Caesar salad dressing

3 cups of romaine lettuce (chopped)

1 loaf of bread

Slices of chicken

Recipe Ingredients:

Place the lettuce in a bowl and cover the lettuce with the Cesar dressing and grated cheese.

Slice the loaf.

Lay the meat slices on the bread.

Place the lettuce on top of the meat.

Layer another piece of bread to finish the sandwiches.

Serving Instructions, Variations and Tips:

This recipe makes 4 servings.

Apple bread works well for this recipe.

If desired, substitute another meat in place of the chicken.

Salmon Salad Sandwich

Recipe Ingredients:

1 tablespoon of lemon juice

1/3 cup of green onions (chopped)

1/3 cup of celery (chopped)

1/3 cup of plain yogurt

7 ounces of canned salmon (drained and flaked)

12 slices bread

Black pepper

Cooking Directions:

Place the flaked salmon in a bowl and add the yogurt, onions, celery, lemon juice and a bit of pepper.

Blend the ingredients.

Spread over 6 slices of bread.

Top with the other 6 pieces of bread.

Serving Instructions, Variations and Tips:

Cut the sandwiches into halves or quarters before serving.

This recipe serves 6 people.

If desired, use crackers in place of bread.

Chicken Bean and Avocado Tortas

Recipe Ingredients:

1/4 cup of pickled jalapeño pepper slices

2/3 cup of black beans (mashed)

1 ripe avocado

1 tomato (sliced)

1 cup of lettuce (shredded)

2 rolls

8 ounces of grilled chicken breast (sliced)

Salt

Black pepper

Cooking Directions:

Cut the avocado in half, twist apart and remove the pit.

Spoon out the pulp and mash the avocado in a bowl.

Cut the rolls in half and spread the avocado over one side of each roll.

Season to taste with a bit of salt and pepper.

Stack the other ingredients on the other side of the roll and press the sandwiches closed.

Serving Instructions, Variations and Tips:

This recipe will serve 2.

In place of rolls, you can use 4 slices of bread.

Avo Bacon Sandwiches

Recipe Ingredients:

1/2 teaspoon of lemon juice

3 tablespoons of butter

4 slices of whole wheat bread

1 ripe avocado

4 slices of bacon

Parsley sprigs

Salt

Pepper

Lemon

Cooking Directions:

Allow the butter to soften at room temperature.

Fry the bacon until it's crisp.

Place the bacon on paper towels and blot off the grease.

Peel the avocado, cut it in half and discard the pit.

Place the avocado, salt, pepper and lemon juice in a bowl and mash the avocado. Blend the ingredients well.

Spread butter onto the bread slices.

Add the avocado mix onto two pieces of bread. Crumble the bacon over the avocado.

Place the other pieces of bread on top to finish the sandwiches.

Serving Instructions, Variations and Tips:

Garnish these sandwiches with a sprig of parsley and a slice of lemon.

These sandwiches make for a great appetizer or finger food when cut into quarters.

If desired, cut off the crusts.

I'm not very fond of bacon or pork (please see my *Healthy Eating Tips* for additional information) but I do realise that many cooks enjoy these items. To ensure your safety and to protect your family from ingesting toxins, I strongly recommend cooking bacon at a very high temperature.

I also recommend organic meats.

Vegetable and Hummus Sandwich

Recipe Ingredients:

2 tablespoons of hummus

2 slices of cheese

2 slices of bread

2 slices of tomato

2 leaves of lettuce

Avocado (sliced)

Vinegar

Olive oil

Cooking Directions:

Spread the hummus on the top of each bread slice.

Layer the other ingredients.

Drizzle oil and vinegar over the veggies and serve.

Serving Instructions, Variations and Tips:

If desired, add other veggies such as onion, carrots, spinach or zucchini.

Spicy Avocado Onion Quesadillas

Recipe Ingredients:

1/4 teaspoon of Tabasco sauce

1/2 teaspoon of vegetable oil

1 tablespoon of red onion (chopped)

2 teaspoons of fresh lemon juice

3 tablespoons of fresh cilantro (chopped)

1/4 cup sour cream

1 1/3 cups of Monterrey Jack cheese (coarsely grated)

1 ripe Haas avocado (peeled and diced)

2 ripe tomatoes (seeded and diced)

4 6-to-7-inch flour tortillas

2 ripe tomatoes (seeded and diced)

Cooking Directions:

Combine the Tabasco sauce, salt, pepper, lemon, onion, tomatoes and avocado in a small bowl.

Blend the cilantro and sour cream.

Preheat your broiler.

Lay the tortillas on a large cookie sheet.

Brush oil over the tortillas.

Broil the tortillas until they're golden brown.

Flip the tortillas and continue to broil. They should be golden brown in color on the second side.

Sprinkle cheese over the tortillas.

Broil until the cheese completely melts.

Spread the avocado mix onto the tortillas and make a quesadilla by placing another tortilla on top, with the cheese side facing the avocado.

Slice the quesadillas into small triangles.

Top each wedge with a heaping teaspoon of sour cream mixture and

Serving Instructions, Variations and Tips:

Garnish this dish with fresh sprigs of cilantro.

Speedy Burgers on the Barbi

Recipe Ingredients:

1/4 teaspoon pepper

1/2 teaspoon of salt

1 tablespoon of prepared mustard

2 tablespoons of flour

6 tablespoons of tomato sauce

1/2 cup of onions (chopped)

1 cup of sour cream

1 pound of ground beef

8 hamburger buns

Cooking Directions:

Place the beef and onion in a pan and brown over medium-high heat.

Mix the salt, pepper, flour, catsup and mustard.

Add the sour cream.

Lightly-toast the hamburger buns.

Serving Instructions, Variations and Tips:

When possible, opt for a sugar-free tomato sauce.

Turkey Pineapple and Avocado Sandwich

Recipe Ingredients:

1/4 teaspoon of prepared horseradish

1 teaspoon of fresh lemon juice

4 teaspoons of honey mustard

1/4 cup of shredded Swiss cheese

1/2 of a ripe avocado (mashed)

4 chunky slices of bread

4 slices of canned pineapple (drained)

8 slices of turkey breast

Cooking Directions:

Lightly toast the bread.

Mix the avocado, horseradish and lemon juice in a small bowl.

Spread the mix over the bread slices.

Place a slice of pineapple and two slices of turkey on each piece of bread.

Apply a small amount of mustard to each sandwich.

Sprinkle cheese over the sandwiches and grill for a few minutes to melt it.

Serving Instructions, Variations and Tips:

Serve warm.

Cheesey Beef Slices

Recipe Ingredients:

2 teaspoons of oil

1 cup of onions (very thinly sliced)

3 slices of mozzarella cheese

6 beef slices (very thinly sliced)

Salt and pepper

French loaf

Cooking Directions:

Preheat your oven to 350 degrees F.

Pour 1 teaspoon of oil into a very hot skillet.

Sear the beef on 30 seconds on each side. The meat should be browned.

Sprinkle salt and pepper over the beef.

Place cheese and the meat on the bread. Put the slices on a baking sheet.

Bake until the cheese melts and the bread is lightly toasted.

Sauté onions in the skillet until they're soft and tender.

Top the sandwich with the onions.

Serving Instructions, Variations and Tips:

If desired, use a gluten-free bread for this recipe.

Lemon Chicken Salad Finger Sandwiches

Recipe Ingredients:

1/4 teaspoon salt

1/2 teaspoon grated lemon zest

1 tablespoon of fresh dill (chopped)

2 teaspoons of lemon juice

1/4 cup of mayonnaise

1/4 cup of plain yogurt

2 cooked whole boneless, skinless chicken breasts

4 lettuce leaves, optional

8 slices bread

Cooking Directions:

Cut the chicken into bite-sized chunks.

Get a medium mixing bowl and combine the chicken, lemon juice, salt, dill, mayonnaise and yogurt.

Add a bit of dressing and toss to make the chicken salad.

Set out the bread slices and place a leaf of lettuce on each.

Spoon the chicken salad onto the lettuce.

Top with a piece of bread and cut the sandwiches into quarters.

Serving Instructions, Variations and Tips:

This recipe makes 16 finger sandwiches.

You can store the chicken salad mix in an air tight container for a couple days.

Spicy Chicken and Avocado Pita Pockets

Recipe Ingredients:
1/4 teaspoon of salt

1/2 teaspoon salt

1 tablespoon of vegetable oil

1 1/2 teaspoons of lemon juice

1/2 cup of sour cream

1/2 cup of taco sauce

1 cup of lettuce (shredded)

2 cups of Monterrey Jack cheese (shredded)

2 cups of cooked chicken (finely chopped)

1 4-ounce can of chopped green chiles (drained)

1 onion, sliced and separated into rings

1 avocado (thinly sliced)

8 pita breads (about 3 1/2 inches in diameter)

Cooking Directions:
Mix the lemon juice and 1/4 teaspoon of salt.

Spritz the lemon juice mix over the avocado slices.

Combine the oil, onion, chiles, chicken and 1/2 teaspoon of salt.

Place approximately 1/4 cup of the mixture into each pita. Sprinkle shredded cheese and lettuce inside the pitas.

Serving Instructions, Variations and Tips:

This recipe serves 8.

You can serve this with sour cream and/or taco sauce.

Tuna Cream Cheese Spread and Crackers

Recipe Ingredients:

1/2 teaspoon of dill weed

2 tablespoons of scallion slices

1 can of flaked tuna (drained)

8 ounces of cream cheese

Cooking Directions:

Allow the cream cheese to soften at room temperature.

Combine the ingredients and gently blend.

Spread the mix over crackers or bread.

Serving Instructions, Variations and Tips:

If desired, lightly grill the bread.

This recipe also works well as a dip.

If desired, add a dash of salt and pepper to taste.

Greek Feta and Olive Quesadilla

Recipe Ingredients:

2 tablespoons of feta cheese

3 tablespoons of diced Kalamata olives

1/8 cup of onion (finely diced)

1/4 cup shredded mozzarella cheese

1 flour tortilla

Oregano

Basil

Rosemary

Cooking Directions:

Distribute the ingredients over the tortilla.

Fold in half.

Grill for about approximately 2 minutes or bake at 350 degrees F for 5 minutes.

Serving Instructions, Variations and Tips:

Slice into thirds and serve.

Fast-prep Beef Sandwiches

Recipe Ingredients:

1 teaspoon of milk

1 teaspoon of prepared horseradish

2 teaspoons of lemon juice

1/4 cup of walnut chunks

3 ounces of cream cheese

1 small apple (finely chopped)

Roast beef (thinly sliced)

Green onions (sliced)

Bread rolls

Lettuce leaves

Cooking Directions:

Spritz the lemon juice over the apple bit.

Mix the milk, horseradish and cream cheese in a small bowl.

Add the apple and walnut to the cream cheese mix.

Spread the cream cheese mix over the bread rolls.

Place a slice of roast beef, onion and lettuce on each roll bottom.

Smoothie Snacks

Smoothies make a great snack, whether it's at home, at work or on-the-go.

Coconut milk makes for a great alternative to cow's milk for individuals who are lactose intolerant. The body processes coconut milk very easily and it's helpful in aiding digestion and in regulating your blood sugars.

Almond milk is another great alternative to dairy milk. It's packed with vitamins and calcium and it's free of cholesterol and saturated fats.

For an added boost, add some milled flax seeds to your smoothie.

High-Protein Fruit Smoothie

Recipe Ingredients:

1 cup of fresh strawberries

1 cup of fresh bananas

1 cup of milk

1 cup of water

3 cups of of ice cubes

2 scoops of whey protein

Cooking Directions:

Mix the ingredients in a blender and serve.

Serving Instructions, Variations and Tips:

Substitute the cow's milk with a dairy-free variety such as almond or coconut milk.

Strawberry, Banana and Honey Smoothie

Recipe Ingredients:

1 teaspoon of honey

1 1/2 tablespoons of flax seed

2 tablespoons of powdered milk

1/2 cup of milk

1/2 cup of strawberries

1/2 cup of plain yogurt

1/2 frozen banana

Cooking Directions:

Peel and chop the banana.

Place the ingredients in a blender and blend until smooth.

Serving Instructions, Variations and Tips:

Substitute the cow's milk with a dairy-free variety such as almond or coconut milk.

Fresh or frozen strawberries will work for this recipe.

Creamy Fruit Smoothie

Recipe Ingredients:

1 tablespoon of milk powder

1/3 cup of blueberries

1/2 cup of orange juice

1 cup of strawberries

1 1/2 cups of plain yogurt

2 bananas

Cooking Directions:

Peel the bananas and chop them into chunks.

Remove the green tops from the strawberries.

Mix up the ingredients in a blender and serve.

Serving Instructions, Variations and Tips:

Dairy milk powder is suitable for this recipe, as are dairy-free varieties such as almond or coconut milk powder.

Fresh or frozen blueberries work for this recipe.

For extra nutrients, add flaxseed or even some spinach. You can't taste it, but your body will benefit.

If desired, use frozen fruit for an icy drink without having to add ice to the recipe.

Speedy-prep Banana Milk Smoothie

Recipe Ingredients:

2 tablespoons of coconut milk powder

1 cup of almond milk

1 banana

Cooking Directions:

Blend the ingredients and serve.

Serving Instructions, Variations and Tips:

If desired, add a sweetener such as honey or stevia.

Speedy, Simple Banana Coconut Smoothie

Recipe Ingredients:

1/4 teaspoon of vanilla flavouring

2 tablespoons of coconut milk powder

1/4 cup of almond milk

1/3 cup of frozen blueberries

1/2 cup of ice cubes

1 large banana

Cooking Directions:

Combine the ingredients in a blender and mix until you achieve a smooth texture.

Serving Instructions, Variations and Tips:

If it's too thick, add a bit of almond milk or water. Thicken with a bit of yogurt.

If desired, use a natural sweetener such as stevia, honey or Luo Han.

Pineapple Yogurt Smoothie

Recipe Ingredients:

1/2 cup of milk

1 cup of pineapple chunks

1 cup of crushed ice
1 1/2 cups of strawberries

1 1/2 cups of plain yogurt

Cooking Directions:
Blend the ingredients until they're smooth.

Serving Instructions, Variations and Tips:

If it's too thick, add a bit of almond milk or water. Thicken with a bit of yogurt.

If desired, use a natural sweetener such as stevia, honey or Luo Han.

Fresh or frozen fruit will work for this recipe.

Speedy Peach Smoothie

Recipe Ingredients:

1 peach

1 cup of plain yogurt

Milk

Ice cubes

Cinnamon

Cooking Directions:

Pour the ingredients into a blender, along with a dash of cinnamon.

Mix well and serve.

Serving Instructions, Variations and Tips:

If it's too thick, add a bit of milk. If it's too runny, simply thicken with a bit of yogurt.

If desired, use Greek yogurt for a creamier, thicker texture.

Peach and Blueberry Pecan Smoothie

Recipe Ingredients:

¼ teaspoon of vanilla

½ teaspoon of salt

½ tablespoon of pecans (crushed)

½ cup of skim milk

6 ounces of vanilla frozen yogurt

1 frozen peach

1 handful of frozen blueberries

Cooking Directions:

Blend the blueberries and peach.

Add the yogurt and blend for a few seconds.

Add the remaining ingredients and blend until it's smooth.

Serving Instructions, Variations and Tips:

If desired, add a dash of salt.

If desired, substitute the vanilla frozen yogurt with plain yogurt and a few drops of vanilla bean flavoring.

Orange Almond Peach Smoothie

Recipe Ingredients:

2 tablespoons of toasted slivered almonds

1 cup of orange juice

1 cup of frozen peaches

1 frozen banana

Cooking Directions:

Place the fruits in the blender, followed by the juice and nuts.

Blend until smooth, then serve.

Serving Instructions, Variations and Tips:

If desired, use pecans in this smoothie.

For a different flavor, use pineapple juice instead of orange.

Miscellaneous

Avocado Tortillas

Recipe Ingredients:

Avocado mashed

Cottage cheese

Lemon juice

Oregano leaves (crushed)

Onion powder

Garlic powder

Soft tortillas

Cooking Directions:

Mash an avocado in a bowl.

Sprinkle avocado with lemon juice to preserve color.

Mix the avocado and cottage cheese in a 3-to-1 combo. Blend thoroughly.

Add the remaining ingredients (except for the tortillas.)

Spoon the mix into the tortillas and roll closed.

Heat on the grill or in the oven for a minute or two to heat throughout.

Serving Instructions, Variations and Tips:

Serve immediately after you're finished preparing the tortillas.

Optional ingredient: Green chillies.

Homemade Hummus

Recipe Ingredients:

½ teaspoon of salt

½ teaspoon of cumin

3 tablespoons of sesame seed paste (tahini)

¼ cup of olive oil

2 cans of chickpeas

2 cloves of garlic

2 lemons squeezed plus 2 tablespoons of water

Cooking Directions:

Mix the tahini, garlic, chickpeas, lemon juice, and water in a food processor.

Blend until smooth.

Add the olive oil, cumin and salt

Blend a bit more.

Serving Instructions, Variations and Tips:

Hummus works best as a veggie dip for carrots, celery, broccoli, cauliflower and cucumber.

Creamy Mushroom Soup

Recipe Ingredients:

Mushrooms

Onions

Garlic cloves (minced)

Heavy whipping cream

Chicken broth

Cornstarch

Swiss cheese

Salt

Pepper

Water

Cooking Directions:

Sauté the garlic, onions and mushrooms.

Warm the chicken broth and cream in a saucepan.

Combine a bit of water and cornstarch in a small bowl, then add it to the saucepan.

Add the cooked mushrooms, onion and garlic to the saucepan and keep it over medium heat.

Stir occasionally until the soup thickens.

Add the Swiss cheese and stir until it melts.

Serving Instructions, Variations and Tips:

Opt for Maitake Mushrooms for an immune boosting meal.
Serve immediately.

Speedy-prep Quesadilla Bites

Recipe Ingredients:

1/2 teaspoon of Dijon mustard

1 tablespoon of green onions (sliced)

1 tablespoon of coriander (chopped)

1/3 cup of cheddar cheese (grated)

1 7-inch soft tortilla

Cooking Directions:

Preheat your oven to 350 degrees F.

Spread the mustard over the tortilla.

Sprinkle the coriander, onions and cheese over the quesadilla.

Roll up the tortilla and wrap it in aluminum foil.

Bake for 12 minutes.

Slice the tortilla roll into bite-sized segments.

Serving Instructions, Variations and Tips:

Each tortilla will make 5 or 6 pieces.

Serve with salsa while warm.

If desired, substitute the coriander with parsley.

Healthy Snacks for Weight Loss

Tips

Fresh veggies are great for dipping, making them ideal after-school snacks or an appetizer. Good dipping vegetables include celery, carrots, slices of peppers, cauliflower and broccoli.

Cherry tomatoes also make a great starter or snack. Simply scoop out the seeds and center and spoon in a bit of veggie dip or a spread.

If desired, roll deli meats around veggies for a healthy dipper.

These snacks are ideal for anyone on a diet. If you avoid carbohydrates, sugar and gluten, you're left with very few elements – namely, fat and protein. These substances are used by the body as fuel; in fact, the body is more efficient at using fat than it is at using carbohydrates. The primary key is moderation.

Cheesy Basil Boursin Dip

Recipe Ingredients:

1 tablespoon of fresh basil

1 tablespoon of fresh dill

8 ounces of cream cheese

2 garlic cloves (peeled)

6 black olives (pitted and chopped)

Cooking Directions:

Place the garlic, herbs and cream cheese in a food processor and blend until it's smooth in consistency.

Mix in the chopped olives.

Serving Instructions, Variations and Tips:

Boursin spread is great for crackers or as a dip for vegetables.

Basil Mozzarella Tomato Salad

Recipe Ingredients:

Mozzarella cheese (sliced)

Basil leaves (chopped)

Beef tomatoes (sliced)

Black Pepper

Olive oil

Balsamic vinegar

Cooking Directions:

Arrange alternating slices of cheese and slices of tomatoes in a dish.

Spritz a few drops of vingar over the tomatoes and cheese.

Drizzle olive oil over the mozzarella and veggies.

Sprinkle a bit of basil and pepper.

Serving Instructions, Variations and Tips:

If desired, add salt to taste.

Reduced fat cheese is suitable for this recipe.

Tuna and Cream Cheese Dip

Recipe Ingredients:

1 6-ounce can of tuna

1 8-ounce brick of cream cheese

Cooking Directions:

Set out the cream cheese and allow it to soften at room temperature.

Drain the tuna. Cut it into flakes.

Mash the cream cheese and blend in the tuna.

Serving Instructions, Variations and Tips:

Use this as a dip or a spread on crackers.

Balsamic Stuffed Mozzarella

Recipe Ingredients:

1 tablespoon of balsamic vinegar

4 ounces of mozzarella cheese

2 cups of salad greens

3/4 pound of fresh spinach (steamed)

2 red bell peppers (sliced lengthwise)

2 tomatoes (sliced)

Cooking Directions:

Work the cheese into ½ inch thickness.

Place peppers and spinach on top of the cheese and roll into a log.

Slice up the log.

Arrange the tomato slices on a dish and pour a bit of vinegar over the veggies.

Serving Instructions, Variations and Tips:

This recipe serves 4 people.

Parmesan Spinach Artichoke Dip

Recipe Ingredients:

1/8 teaspoon of garlic powder

1/4 teaspoon of salt

1/2 teaspoon of red pepper flakes (crushed)

1/2 cup of spinach (chopped)

1/2 cup of Parmesan cheese (grated)

1 cup of artichoke hearts (chopped)

8 ounces of cream cheese

Black pepper

Cooking Directions:

Place the spinach and artichoke hearts in a saucepan with water. Boil over medium heat for approximately 10 minutes. They must be soft and tender.

Place the cream cheese and Parmesan in a small saucepan and warm it over medium heat until it's melted and warm.

Stir the ingredients into the cheese. Blend well.

Serving Instructions, Variations and Tips:

This recipe will serve 4.

Serve hot with chips or crackers.

Frozen and thawed or canned artichoke works well for this recipe. If you're using canned artichokes, drain away the liquid before preparing this dish.

Seasoned Toasty Nuts

Recipe Ingredients:

1/4 teaspoon of cayenne pepper

1/2 teaspoon of garlic powder

1/2 teaspoon of sale

1 teaspoon of seasoned salt

1 teaspoon of seasoned pepper

2 tablespoons of butter

1 cup of whole almonds

1 cup of pecan halves

1 cup of walnut halves

Cooking Directions:

Preheat your oven to 300 degrees F.

Melt the butter in large skillet.

Stir in the nuts and spices.

Place the ingredients in a baking sheet and cook in the oven for 10 minutes.

Remove the pan after 10 minutes and stir.

Bake for an additional 10 minutes. The ingredients should be lightly toasted.

Serving Instructions, Variations and Tips:

Store the cooled nuts in an air-tight container.

Simple Stuffed Mushrooms

Recipe Ingredients:

4 ounces of cream cheese

Dried beef

Whole mushrooms

Cooking Directions:

Preheat your oven to 350 degrees F.

Allow the cream cheese to soften at room temperature.

Remove the mushroom stems and rinse out the tops.

Chop the dried beef into small chunks and blend into the cream cheese.

Blend the beef with the cream cheese.

Spoon the cream cheese mix into the mushroom caps and set on a baking sheet.

Bake for for a few minutes. The cheese should be lightly browned.

Serving Instructions, Variations and Tips:

This dish is low in carbohydrate, making it great for dieters.

Simple Guacamole

Recipe Ingredients:
1/8 teaspoon of pepper

2 tablespoons of fresh lemon juice

1 tomato (peeled)

1 garlic clove (finely chopped)

1 small onion (finely chopped)

2 ripe avocados

Himalayan salt

Cooking Directions:
Mash up the tomato in a bowl. A potato masher works well.

Cut the avocados in half and remove the skin and pits.

Blend the avocado flesh with the mashed tomatoes.

Mince the onion and garlic (plus chillies if you are using).

Mix in the onion, lemon juice, garlic and a dash of salt.

Cover and chill in the refrigerator for 1 hour.

Serving Instructions, Variations and Tips:
Black or green avocados work for this dish.

Optional ingredient: If you enjoy spicy foods, add 3 tablespoons of finely chopped green chillies.

If desired, use lime juice in place of lemon juice.

Guacamole will hold for about 1 week.

Speedy and Simple Potato Skins

Recipe Ingredients:

3 russet potatoes

Tuna dip or guacamole

Cooking Directions:

Bake the potatoes.

Slice the cooled potatoes lengthwise.

Scoop out most of the potato (save it to make mashed potatoes!)

Spoon tuna dip or guacamole into the skins.

Serving Instructions, Variations and Tips:

Potato skins are high in fiber.

Opt for organic, pesticide-free potatoes for this dish.

Potato skins go well with a salad or they make a great appetizer.

Homemade Hot Cocoa

Recipe Ingredients:

1 tablespoons of cocoa powder

1 teaspoon of stevia

1/4 cup of cream

3/4 cup of boiling water

Cooking Directions:

Add the water to the cocoa.

Stir in the remaining ingredients.

Serving Instructions, Variations and Tips:

If desired, substitute the stevia with another natural sweetener.

Cheesey Garlic Biscuits

Recipe Ingredients:

1 teaspoon of garlic powder

1 1/2 teaspoon of butter

2 tablespoons of baking powder

1/8 cup of oil

1/4 cup of water

1/2 cup of cream

1 1/2 cup of whey protein powder

3 ounces of cheddar cheese (grated)

3 eggs (beaten)

Cooking Directions:

Preheat your oven to 350 degrees F.

Combine the ingredients and work into a dough consistency.

Spoon the dough onto a baking sheet.

Bake the biscuits for approximately 10 to 15 minutes. They should be light golden brown in color.

Serving Instructions, Variations and Tips:

This recipe will make 18 biscuits.

Add the water gradually and mix to avoid making the mix too thin.

Hearty Almond Muffins

Recipe Ingredients:

2 teaspoon of baking powder

1 tablespoons of cream

2 tablespoons of ground almonds

3 tablespoons of sour cream

3 tablespoons of melted butter

4 tablespoons of flax seeds

2 scoops of protein powder

2 large eggs

Cooking Directions:

Preheat oven to 350 degrees F.

Grind the seeds until they reach a meal consistency.

Mix the dry ingredients in a mixing bowl.

Combine the remaining ingredients in a second bowl.

Combine the contents of the two bowls and blend well.

Grease a couple muffin tins.

Bake the muffins for approximately 20 to 25 minutes.

Serving Instructions, Variations and Tips:

The recipe makes 6 muffins.

Optional ingredient: 1 teaspoon of almond extract.

Allow them to cool for 5 minutes before moving the muffins to a cooling rack.

Mediterranean Mushroom Salad

Recipe Ingredients:

1 teaspoon of basil and marjoram

1 tablespoon of olive oil

1 tablespoon of fresh parsley

3 tablespoons of lemon juice

1/2 cup of water

1/2 pound of mushrooms

1 medium tomato (diced)

3 cloves of garlic (finely chopped)

Salt

Black pepper

Cooking Directions:

Pour the oil in a frying pan and heat it on low.

Place the mushrooms in the pan and fry them for approximately 2 to 3 minutes.

Add the basil and garlic and mix until you completely coat the mushrooms.

Stir in the remaining ingredients. Cook until the tomato is soft and slightly tender.

Remove from heat and allow it to cool before serving.

Serving Instructions, Variations and Tips:

This recipe serves 6.

Garnish with chopped herbs.

If desired, use coriander in place of parsley.

Use caution to avoid over-cooking the mushrooms.

Asparagus Avocado Salad

Recipe Ingredients:

2 tablespoons of Italian dressing

1 avocado

1 sweet red pepper

¾ pound of thin asparagus spears

Red leaf lettuce

Cooking Directions:

Steam the asparagus. They should be crisp and bright green in color.

Place the asparagus under cold running water immediately after steaming.

Peel the avocado and remove the pit.

Cut the avocado halves into 6 slices.

Cut off the top and bottom of the pepper and cut the remaining straight side portions into thin strips.

Chop the top and bottoms of the peppers into fine bits.

Place a couple lettuce leaves on a serving dish.

Create a pinwheel shape using the asparagus and peppers. Use the chopped asparagus for the centers.

Drizzle some dressing over the veggies.

Place the avocado where the slices of pepper and asparagus meet.

Serving Instructions, Variations and Tips:

This recipe serves 2.

You can use vinaigrette dressing in place of Italian. You can also opt for butter lettuce in place of red leaf lettuce.

Speedy-prep Curry Chicken Salad

Recipe Ingredients:

2 tablespoons of curry powder

1/4 cup of chopped walnuts

1/2 cup of mayonnaise

2 cups of cooked chicken (diced)

1 1/2 sticks of celery (chopped)

Cooking Directions:

Combine the ingredients in a salad bowl and blend.

Serving Instructions, Variations and Tips:

This dish is a fast easy lunch dish or a great dinner, especially if you're running late.

Homemade Cream of Mushroom Soup

Recipe Ingredients:
2 cups of heavy cream

1/2 chicken bouillon cube

1 large can of mushrooms

Parsley flakes

Cooking Directions:
Place the ingredients in a food processor or blender and blend on low until it reaches a smooth consistency.

Pour the soup into saucepan. Cover it and simmer on low heat.

Stir occasionally and cook until it's hot, just before it boils.

Serving Instructions, Variations and Tips:
This recipe serves 2 people.

Simple Chicken Cabbage Soup

Recipe Ingredients:

1 large head of green cabbage

1 tomato

1 bunch of celery

2 chicken breasts (skinless

3 turnips

6 chicken bullion cubes

Water

Cooking Directions:

Slice up the ingredients so they're all in small, bite-sized chunks.

Place the ingredients in a 2-quart pot and fill it with water.

Boil on the stove until the cabbage is soft and tender.

Zucchini Onion Hash

Recipe Ingredients:

1 tablespoons of onion (grated)

1 cup of zucchini (grated)

2 eggs (lightly beaten)

Salt

Pepper

Onion powder

Cooking Directions:

Heat a bit of oil in skillet.

Combine the ingredients in a bowl.

Spoon the ingredients into the skillet (gradually to avoid splashing hot oil).

Brown the ingredients on both sides.

Serving Instructions, Variations and Tips:

Use gravy, sour cream or butter as a topping.

If desired, add a bit of garlic powder to this dish.

This is a low-carb meal, ideal for dieters!

If necessary, cook this dish in batches.

Simple Baked Butternut Squash

Recipe Ingredients:

1 tablespoon of butter

1/2 stick of butter

1 butternut squash

1 large sweet onion

Cooking Directions:

Preheat your oven to 400 degrees F.

Cut the squash in half and remove the seeds.

Place the squash halves upside down in a baking pan and for approximately 40 to 50 minutes. They should be soft and tender.

Remove the interior of the squash halves and combine it with butter in a bowl.

Sauté onions in a bit of butter and mix it into the squash.

Serving Instructions, Variations and Tips:

This recipe will make 6 to 8 servings.

If desired, roast the seeds for a separate snack.

Serve the squash warm.

This recipe will take a while to cook, but it's very easy and simple to prepare. So it's ideal for the weekend or evenings.

Fat Burning
Foods Snacks

Blueberries

Blueberries aren't just easy to eat on the run as a snack. They're also considered a "super food" that's high in anti oxidants and low in calories. They're even believed to help you eliminate fat deposits around your mid-section.

Blueberries contain lots of phytonutrients, which release beneficial enzymes. Antioxidants serve to combat free radicals, which if left in place, can lead to illness and disease.

Blueberries are also low in sugar, making them ideal for anyone who is seeking to lower their sugar intake.

Carrots

Simply digesting raw carrots will burn more calories than are contained in the veggie! Therefore, this is one vegetable that's known as a "negative calorie food." Celery is another negative calorie food.

What's more, carrots are full of vitamins and minerals, and they'll leave you feeling full, which helps you eat less of other, high-calorie foods. So if you're looking to lose weight, add carrots to your arsenal!

Cherries

Cherries are packed with antioxidants, vitamins and other beneficial nutrients. In fact, this low-fat food serves to help lower your cholesterol.

Cherries are also useful for keeping your blood sugar up and speeding your metabolism, thereby promoting weight loss. Research has also revealed that they contain an antioxidant called anthocyanin, which is believed to be effective in eliminating belly fat.

High in fibre and potassium, cherries can also serve to help you burn fat, while controlling your body's water levels.

Green beans

Green beans are high in Vitamin C, Protein, iron, fibre, minerals and other nutrients, but they're also low in calories.

Even better? Iron and Vitamin C help promote weight loss!

An Arizona State University study revealed that these nutrients serve to increase the body's ability to burn fat for energy.

Low iron levels can lead to anemia, which leaves you feeling weak, fatigued and prone to opportunistic illnesses. So eat your green beans!

Leeks

Leeks help to stabilize your blood sugar, thereby reducing cravings while making you feel more energized!

Leeks are packed with vitamins and other nutrients. In parts of Europe such as France, they're often eaten in soup, which is very low calorie with just 50 calories in a cup!

Pears

Pears are free of sodium, saturated fat and cholesterol, making this a great fruit for dieters.

Pears are extremely high in fibre, which makes you feel full so you'll eat less of those other, high-calorie and high-fat foods. Even better, pears serve to moderate your blood sugar levels and they can lower "bad" cholesterol levels.

Healthy Snacks for Kids

Vegetable Snacks

Veggie Waffle Sandwich

Recipe Ingredients:

2 tomato slices

2 frozen waffles

4 cucumber slices

Shredded carrots

Ranch dressing

Cooking Directions:

Toast the waffles to your preference.

Spread ranch dressing onto each waffle.

Place the cucumber and carrot slices on one of the waffles.

Sprinkle shredded carrots over top of the ingredients.

Place the remaining waffle on top.

Serving Instructions, Variations and Tips:

Cut the waffles into quarters.

If desired, use a different type of dressing or alternative veggies for a different flavor.

Chips and Bean Salsa Dip

Recipe Ingredients:

2/3 cup of salsa

1 cup of refried beans

1 bag of baked potato chips

Cooking Directions:

Pour the beans and salsa into a mixing bowl.

Mix up the ingredients.

Use the salsa-bean blend as a dip for the chips.

Serving Instructions, Variations and Tips:

If desired, make your own salsa and chips for a healthier dish.

Cheesey Broccoli Balls

Recipe Ingredients:

1 cup of bread crumbs

1 cup of cheddar cheese (shredded)

16 ounces of frozen broccoli

3 eggs

Oil

Cooking Directions:

Preheat your oven to 375 degrees F.

Cook the broccoli according to package directions.

Pour the broccoli into a colander to drain away the water.

Chop the broccoli into small chunks.

Place the eggs, cooked broccoli, bread crumbs and cheese in a large bowl and mix gently with your hands.

Apply a bit of oil to a baking sheet.

Roll the mixture into small balls and place them on the baking sheet.

Bake the balls for 20 minutes.

Remove the baking sheet and flip the balls.

Bake for a additional 10 minutes.

Serving Instructions, Variations and Tips:

If desired, use Swiss cheese in place of cheddar.

Hidden Veggie Brownies

Recipe Ingredients:

1/2 teaspoon of baking powder

1/2 teaspoon of salt

2 teaspoons of vanilla

2 tablespoons of margarine

1/4 cup of unsweetened cocoa powder

1/2 cup of carrot puree

1/2 cup of spinach puree

1/2 cup of brown sugar

3/4 cup all purpose flour

3 ounces of dark chocolate

2 egg whites

Oil

Cooking Directions:

Preheat your oven to 350 degrees F.

Set out the margarine and allow it to soften at room temperature.

Boil a pan of water and place a glass bowl over the top.

Melt the chocolate in the bowl.

Stir in the spinach puree, brown sugar, margarine, carrot, cocoa powder and vanilla with the melted chocolate. Stir until the mix is well-blended and creamy in consistency.

Separate the egg yolk from the whites and whisk the egg whites.

Pour in the salt, baking powder and flour with the egg. Mix well and combine with the other ingredients.

Butter a baking pan.

Pour the mix into a pan and bake for approximately 30 minutes. To test to determine if the brownies are done stick a toothpick or skewer into the brownies. It should come up clean when you remove it. If the mix sticks, bake for a bit longer.

Serving Instructions, Variations and Tips:

Allow the brownies to cool before you cut them and serve.

If possible, opt for naturally sweetened dark chocolate.

For a healthier recipe, opt for a natural sweetener such as stevia and a reduced-fat margarine.

This is an easy way to get your kids to eat veggies, as you cannot taste them in the brownies.

Cheesey Zucchini Strips

Recipe Ingredients:

1/4 cup of Parmesan cheese

1/3 cup of seasoned bread crumbs

1 egg

4 small zucchinis

Oil

Cooking Directions:

Preheat your oven to 450 degrees F.

Cut the zucchinis lengthwise into thin, easy-to-bite "finger" strips.

Place the egg in a bowl and beat with a whisk.

Place the cheese and bread crumbs in a separate bowl.

Dip the slices of zucchini into the egg mixture, then dip into the cheese and bread crumb mix to coat them.

Oil a baking sheet and place the zucchini chunks onto the sheet.

Bake the zucchini for approximately 20 minutes. They should be soft, tender and golden brown in color.

Serving Instructions, Variations and Tips:

These zucchini strips go well with a veggie dip.

Cinnamon Sweet Potato and Oat Squares

Recipe Ingredients:

2 tablespoons of cinnamon

2 tablespoons of coconut oil

1/4 cup of brown sugar

2/3 cup of maple syrup

2/3 cup of orange juice

4 cups of fast-cook oats

5 sweet potatoes

Cooking Directions:

Preheat your oven to 400 degrees F.

Cook the sweet potatoes until they're soft and tender.

Cut them in half the long way and scoop out the pulp.

Combine the potato pulp with cinnamon, brown sugar, orange juice, oil and maple syrup.

Mix well and stir in the oats.

Lightly grease a large baking dish.

Pour mixture into prepared dish and bake for approximately 20 minutes. You'll know it's done when you can poke it with a skewer or toothpick and it will come out clean.

Serving Instructions, Variations and Tips:

Cool before cutting into squares.

Cinnamon Squash Muffins

Recipe Ingredients:

1/2 teaspoon of baking soda

1/2 teaspoon of salt

1 teaspoon of nutmeg

1 1/2 teaspoons of cinnamon

2 teaspoons of baking powder

2 tablespoons of canola oil

1 cup of brown sugar

1 cup of butternut squash

2 1/2 cups of flour

2 eggs

Cooking Directions:

Steam and mash the squash. Measure out 1 cup.

Preheat your the oven to 400 degrees F.

In a bowl, blend the salt, nutmeg, cinnamon, flour, baking soda and baking powder.

Use an electric mixer to beat the sugar and butter in a second bowl. It must be creamy in consistency.

Add the squash and eggs to the butter-sugar mix and mix well.

Mix in the dry ingredients. Stir until the mix is soft and well-blended.

Place muffin papers in a tin.

Pour the mix into each muffin cup. Fill each ¾ of the way to accommodate expansion during baking.

Bake the muffins for approximately 15 minutes. When they're done, they'll be soft but not mushy. The muffin will bounce back when you press on the top.

Serving Instructions, Variations and Tips:

Allow the muffins to cool for a few minutes before you serve.

If desired, use gluten-free coconut flour instead, but beware that you'll need to use less since it tends to expand a bit.

These muffins go well with honey!

Cottage Cheese Stuffed Cherry Tomatoes

Recipe Ingredients:

1/4 teaspoon of onion powder

1 teaspoon of mustard

1 teaspoon of celery salt

1 cup of cottage cheese

30 cherry tomatoes

Cooking Directions:

Cut off the cherry tomato tops.

Spoon out the seeds.

Mix the cottage cheese, onion powder, mustard and celery salt in a bowl. Blend well.

Spoon the mix into each cherry tomato.

Serving Instructions, Variations and Tips:

Cover and refrigerate these stuffed cherry tomatoes until you're ready to serve.

These stuffed tomatoes make a great snack, party platter or appetizer.

Plain or small curd cottage cheese will work for this dish.

Fruit Snacks for Kids

Blackberry and Banana Milkshake

Recipe Ingredients:

1 pint of milk

1 pint of fresh blackberries

1 firm banana (chopped)

6 ice cubes

Sugar substitute

Vanilla essence

Cooking Directions:

Pour the milk into the blender.

Add the ice, blackberries and bananas.

Blend the mix until it's smooth.

Add the sugar substitute and blend for a moment.

Serving Instructions, Variations and Tips:

Serve immediately.

Sugar substitutes include stevia and honey

Creamy Vanilla Fruit Dippers

Recipe Ingredients:

1 tablespoon of a sugar substitute

1 teaspoon of vanilla extract

6 ounces of vanilla yogurt

8 ounces of cream cheese, room temperature

Strawberries (quartered)

Watermelon (cubed)

Muskmelon (cubed)

Bananas (chunked)

Grapes

Cooking Directions:

Set out the cream cheese and allow it to soften at room temperature.

Combine the cream cheese with the vanilla extract and yogurt.

Use an electric mixer to blend the dip. It should be smooth and creamy in consistency.

Stir in the sugar substitute.

Place the dip in a bowl at the center of a dish and arrange the veggies around the dip.

Serving Instructions, Variations and Tips:

This recipe makes 16 servings.

If desired, spear the fruits with toothpicks for easy dipping.

Sugar substitutes include stevia and honey.

Opt for a fat-free cream cheese and yogurt to cut the calorie count.

Drinkable Fruit Cups

Recipe Ingredients:

1 teaspoon of lemon juice

1 teaspoon of honey

1/4 cup of plain yogurt

1 cup of orange juice

1 banana (sliced)

1 kiwi (peeled and sliced)

6 strawberries (sliced)

Cooking Directions:

Combine the orange juice and yogurt in a mixing bowl.

Stir in the lemon juice and honey.

Mix in the fruit and blend well.

Serving Instructions, Variations and Tips:

This recipe will make 2 servings.

Use a ladle to serve the fruit into into individual cups or bowls.

If desired, experiment with alternative juice types and other varieties of fruit.

Peachy Vanilla Parfait With Granola

Recipe Ingredients:

2 cups of vanilla yogurt

2 cups of granola

2 cups of fresh peaches (chopped)

Cooking Directions:

Divide the yogurt into 4 cups.

Spoon the peaches on top of the yogurt.

Sprinkle granola over the peaches.

Layer the ingredients in the above-mentioned order until you've used up all of the ingredients.

Serving Instructions, Variations and Tips:

This recipe will make 4 servings.

For a slightly different flavor try nuts or dry cereal instead of or in addition to the granola.

If desired, experiment with other varieties of fruit.

Mango Pineapple Orange Creamsicles

Recipe Ingredients:

1/4 cup of pineapple orange juice concentrate

1/2 cup of evaporated milk

¾ cup of water

2 cups of ripe mango (chunked)

Cooking Directions:

Combine the ingredients in a blender.

Blend until the mixture is smooth and creamy in consistency.

Pour the mix into a popsicle mold and insert the popsicle sticks.

Freeze the mixture. It will take approximately 3 to 4 hours for them to freeze.

Serving Instructions, Variations and Tips:

This recipe will make 8 servings.

Kids and adults alike will enjoy these on a hot summer day or any other time of year!

If you don't have a popsicle mold, use 5-ounce paper cups. If you use cups, wait until the popsicles are slushy before you add the sticks.

Strawberry Banana Boat

Recipe Ingredients:

1 teaspoon of raisins

2 teaspoons of strawberry preserves

1 banana

Whipped topping

Cooking Directions:

Peel the banana and cut it down the center.

Position the banana halves in a long sundae dish.

Spoon strawberry preserves into the area between the bananas.

Sprinkle raisins over the preserves.

Top with whipped cream or serve as a side.

Serving Instructions, Variations and Tips:

This recipe makes 1 serving.

Try pineapple preserves and chopped strawberries for a slightly different flavor.

If desired, use nuts in place of raisins.

Peanut Butter Banana Hot Dog

Recipe Ingredients:

2 tablespoons of creamy peanut butter

2 tablespoons of strawberry jam

4 bananas

4 hot dog buns

Cooking Directions:

Spread the peanut butter into each of the hot dog buns.

Peel the bananas and place them in the hot dogs.

Spoon a bit of jam on top of the bananas.

Serving Instructions, Variations and Tips:

This recipe makes 4 servings.

If desired, use nuts or sunflower seeds as a topping. You can also try crunchy peanut butter or alternative flavors of jam.

Granola and Peanut Butter Apples

Recipe Ingredients:

2 tablespoons of peanut butter

1/2 cup of granola

1/2 cup of raisins

4 large apples (cored)

Cooking Directions:

Combine the raisins and peanut butter. Mix well.

Spoon the mixture into the cored apples.

Add granola on top of the mixture.

Serving Instructions, Variations and Tips:

This recipe makes 4 servings.

If desired, use nuts or sunflower seeds as a topping. You can also try crunchy peanut butter.

Alternatively, cut the apples into slices and spread the mix over the slices. Sprinkle granola over the top.

Honey-covered Fruit Cones

Recipe Ingredients:

4 teaspoon of honey

4 teaspoon of pecans (chopped)

1/2 cup of fresh strawberries (chunked)

1/2 cup of fresh pineapple (chunked)

1/2 cup of fresh peaches (chunked)

1/2 cup of banana (chunked)

1/2 cup of fresh blueberries

1/2 cup of fresh raspberries

4 ice cream cones

Cooking Directions:

Mix the fruits in a large bowl.

Spoon the fruit into the cones.

Drizzle honey over the fruit.

Top the honey-covered fruit with nuts.

Serving Instructions, Variations and Tips:

This recipe makes 4 servings.

If desired, use chocolate chips in place of pecans.

Cinnamon Oatmeal Cherry Blend

Recipe Ingredients:

1/2 teaspoon of cinnamon

1 teaspoon of nutmeg

2 teaspoons of vanilla extract

1/3 cup of oil

2/3 cup of dried cherries

2/3 cup of pine nuts (toasted)

3/4 cup of coconut (shredded)

3/4 cup of honey

1 cup of wheat germ

1 cup of cold milled flax

4 cups of old fashioned oatmeal

Cooking Directions:

Preheat your oven to 350 degrees F.

Combine the flax, wheat germ, nutmeg, cinnamon and oatmeal, along with nuts and coconut.

Stir the mix and pour in the vanilla extract, honey and oil.

Mix the contents of the two bowls with a spatula. The dry ingredients must be completely coated.

Use a rubber spatula to stir until all the dry ingredients becomes completely coated.

Oil a large baking sheet and spread the mixture across the

sheet.

Bake for approximately 30 minutes. You must stir the mix every 10 minutes.

Stir in the cherries once baking is complete. Be sure to break up any chunks or lumps.

Serving Instructions, Variations and Tips:

This recipe makes 16 servings.

This mix works well as a topping for fruits, ice cream or frozen yogurt!

Allow the mixture to cool before serving.

Store the cherry mix in an airtight container. It will keep for approximately 1 week.

Butterscotch Pear Ice Cream Topping

Recipe Ingredients:

1 tablespoon of butter

1/2 cup butterscotch ice cream topping

3 ripe pears

Vanilla ice cream

Cooking Directions:

Peel, core and cut the pears into thin slices.

Place the butter in a medium skillet and warm over medium-low heat.

Place the pears in the skillet and cook until they're soft. Stir periodically.

Pour the topping into the skillet and cook until it's warm.

Serve over vanilla ice cream

Serving Instructions, Variations and Tips:

This recipe makes 4 servings.

If desired, use caramel ice cream topping instead.

Speedy-prep Apple Sauce

Recipe Ingredients:

1/3 cup of water

4 small apples

Cinnamon

Nutmeg

Cooking Directions:

Peel and core the apples.

Rinse the apples and slice them into small chunks.

Place the apples in a 2-quart casserole dish.

Add water and cover the dish.

Cook for approximately 5 to 7 minutes. The apples must be soft but not too mushy.

Mix in the cinnamon and nutmeg.

Serving Instructions, Variations and Tips:

This recipe makes 4 servings.

Allow the sauce to sit for 5 minutes before serving. It can also be served cold.

Sandwich Snacks for Kids

Chicken Avocado Sandwich

Recipe Ingredients:

1 teaspoon of salt

3/4 cup of garlic

6 California avocados

16 eggs (beaten)

24 slices of firm sandwich bread

24 slices of Jalapeno Jack cheese

48 slices of roasted chicken or turkey (3 pound)

Mayonnaise or butter

Unsalted butter

Cooking Directions:

Spread mayo or butter on each piece of bread.

Place avocado slices over 12 slices of bread

Place 4 slices of meat and 2 slices of cheese on each sandwich.

Top with another piece of bread and cut diagonally.

Whisk the milk, salt and egg in a bowl.

Dip the sandwich halves in the mix.

Cook for approximately 2 minutes per side.

Serving Instructions, Variations and Tips:

This recipe makes 12 servings.

This sandwich goes well with fruit salsa.

If you're cooking for adults, garnish with a sprig of cilantro.

If desired, use turkey in place of chicken.

Frankburgers Delight

Recipe Ingredients:

1 1/2 tablespoons of Worcestershire sauce

1/4 cup of vinegar

1/2 cup of catsup

1/2 cup of water

1/2 cup of onions (chopped)

1/2 cup of green bell pepper (chopped)

1 pound of hot dogs

Hot dog buns

Cooking Directions:

Preheat your oven to 350 degrees F.

Place the hot dogs in a glass dish.

Combine the sauce, water, peppers, onions, catsup and vinegar.

Pour the mix over the hot dogs.

Bake the hot dogs for 1 hour.

Serve in hot dog buns.

Serving Instructions, Variations and Tips:

This is not a healthy meal, but it's a nice treat for kids.

Whenever possible, opt for the healthier ingredients.

If desired, use hamburger patties and hamburger buns in

place of hot dogs and hot dog buns.

If desired, use tomato sauce in place of catsup.

Very Green Benedictine Sandwich

Recipe Ingredients:

1 pound of cream cheese

1 medium onion

2 cucumbers (peeled)

3 drops of green food coloring

Bread

Cooking Directions:

Grate the onion and cucumber and onion.

Drain away the excess liquid.

Combine the cream cheese with the veggies and a bit of food coloring.

Blend the ingredients in a food processor.

Spread over bread.

Serving Instructions, Variations and Tips:

This recipe makes 2 cups.

If desired, you can use this as a dip or as a cherry tomato stuffing.

Egg Tuna Muffin Sandwich

Recipe Ingredients:

3 tablespoons of margarine

1/8 cup of pecans

1/4 cup of mayonnaise

1 can of tuna (drained)

1 stalk of celery (finely chopped)

2 hard-boiled eggs (chopped)

6 stuffed olives (chopped)

6 English muffins

Cooking Directions:

Slice English muffins lengthwise.

Toast, then butter.

Mix all ingredients and put between the muffins.

Serving Instructions, Variations and Tips:

This recipe makes 12 servings.

Some kids may not like the olives and celery, so you may wish to skip these ingredients.

Cucumber Mayo Sandwiches

Recipe Ingredients:

1 tablespoon of mayonnaise

8 ounces of cream cheese

1 package of Blue Cheese Dressing mix

3 large cucumbers

Bread

Cooking Directions:

Set out the cream cheese and allow it to soften at room temperature.

Shred the cucumbers and drain away extra fluid.

Combine the cheese, mayo and dressing mix.

Add the cucumbers.

Spoon the mix onto bread.

Serving Instructions, Variations and Tips:

You can also serve this on crackers instead of bread.

Simple Egg Salad Sandwiches

Recipe Ingredients:

1/4 cup of fresh basil (cut into strips)

1/2 cup of red sweet onions (diced)

1 teaspoon fresh ground black pepper

1 1/2 teaspoons of Himalayan salt

1 cup of mayonnaise

3 garlic cloves (finely minced)

8 eggs

Cooking Directions:

Boil the eggs for 10 minutes.

Place the eggs in ice water and allow them to cool for 15 minutes.

Remove the shells.

Cut up the eggs and combine the ingredients.

Spread the mix onto toast or plain bread.

Serving Instructions, Variations and Tips:

Some children may prefer a simpler variation with eggs, mayo and black pepper.

Banana and Peanut Butter Sandwich

Recipe Ingredients:

2 tablespoons of butter

3 tablespoons of peanut butter

1 small ripe banana

2 slices of bread

Cooking Directions:

Mash up the banana in a bowl.

Lightly toast 2 slices of bread.

Spread the banana mash on one piece of bread and peanut butter on the other piece of bread.

Close the sandwich and fry on low heat. The bread should be light golden brown in color.

Serving Instructions, Variations and Tips:

Serve this sandwich while it's hot.

Pecan Banana Sandwich

Recipe Ingredients:

1/4 cup of grape pulp

1/2 cup of pecans (chopped)

1 banana

1 orange

Cooking Directions:

Combine the ingredients in a bowl and blend well.

Spoon onto bread and enjoy.

Serving Instructions, Variations and Tips:

Use buttered bread for this sandwich.

Smoothie Snacks for Kids

Banana and Peanut Butter Smoothie

Recipe Ingredients:

1 teaspoon of honey

1 teaspoon of vanilla

1 tablespoon of peanut butter

1 tablespoons of cocoa powder

2 bananas

Greek yogurt

Cooking Directions:

Combine the ingredients and blend.

Serving Instructions, Variations and Tips:

If desired, alter the ingredients or quantities to suit your taste.

Green Berry Smoothie

Recipe Ingredients:

1 cup of blueberries

1 cup of raspberries

2 cups of of water

1 apple

3 handfuls of baby spinach

Cooking Directions:

Blend the berries, apple and water on high until it's smooth.

Add the spinach and blend on high.

Serving Instructions, Variations and Tips:

Kids typically can't taste the spinach in this healthy treat!

Creamy Banana Smoothie

Recipe Ingredients:

1 teaspoon of vanilla extract

12 teaspoons of milk powder

1 cup of milk

1 banana

4 ice cubes

Cooking Directions:

Peel and slice the banana.

Combine the ingredients in the blender.

Blend until smooth and serve.

Serving Instructions, Variations and Tips:

If desired, add a bit of honey or another natural sweetener.

Creamy Orange Smoothie

Recipe Ingredients:

1 teaspoon of vanilla flavoring

¼ cup of orange juice concentrate

¾ cup of milk

1 cup of plain yogurt

Cooking Directions:

Place the ingredients in the blender and mix on high.

Serving Instructions, Variations and Tips:

If desired, use vanilla frozen yogurt in place of plain yogurt.

Banana Berry Smoothie

Recipe Ingredients:

Raspberries

Blackberries

Strawberries

Plain yogurt

1 banana

Apple juice

Cooking Directions:

Peel and slice the banana.

Add all the ingredients and blend.

Serving Instructions, Variations and Tips:

If desired, alter the ingredients and quantities to taste.

You can use fresh or frozen berries for this recipe.

Gluten-Free Snacks

Homemade Gluten-free Granola

Recipe Ingredients:

1 teaspoon of sea salt

1 tablespoon of vanilla extract

1/2 cup of rice bran

1/2 cup of sesame seeds

1/2 cup of flax seeds

1 cup of quinoa flakes

1 cup of coconut flakes

1 cup of coconut oil

1 cup of honey

1 cup of walnuts (chopped)

1 cup of pecans (chopped)

1 cup of almonds (chopped)

1 cup of sunflower seeds

7 cups of gluten-free oats

3 tablespoons of ground cinnamon

Cooking Directions:

Preheat your oven to 350 degrees F.

Mix the dry ingredients in a large bowl.

Combine the oil, honey, and vanilla extract. Mix well.

Mix the dry and we ingredients and blend well.

Press the granola into a lightly-greased pan.

Roast for 10 minutes at 350 degrees.

Mix the granola and cook for another 10 minutes.

Pull the baking sheet out of the oven and allow it to cool to 250 degrees F.

Blend the granola again and bake for another 5 minutes.

Blend in the dry fruit and bake for 10 minutes longer.

Allow it to cool in the baking pan. Stir periodically to prevent clumps.

Serving Instructions, Variations and Tips:

If desired, add buckwheat or millet flakes.

Homemade Gluten-free Granola Bars

Recipe Ingredients:

1/2 teaspoon of cinnamon (ground)

1/2 teaspoon of sea salt

1 teaspoon of vanilla extract

1/4 cup of creamy brown rice farina

1/4 cup of coconut oil

1/2 cup of pecans

2/3 cup of apple sauce

1 cup of apple juice

1 1/2 cups of gluten free flour

2 cups of gluten-free rolled oats

Honey

Cooking Directions:

Preheat your oven to 375 degrees F.

Grease a large pan with oil.

Combine the oats, cinnamon, flour, oats, rice farina and salt in a mixing bowl.

Combine the apple juice, oil, honey, apple sauce and vanilla in a second bowl.

Combine the contents of the two bowls and add pecans.

Blend well and spread the mix into the pan.

Spread mixture into the oiled pan and smooth with the bottom of a spatula.
Bake for 30 minutes.

Allow the pan to cool slightly.

Cut the bars and replace them in the oven.

Bake for 10 additional minutes.

Allow them to cool before serving.

Serving Instructions, Variations and Tips:

Bars store well in a sealed container and also freeze well.

If desired, use molasses or stevia in place of honey, or go without extra sweeteners.

Avocado Seed Dip

Recipe Ingredients:

1 avocado

1 onion (sliced)

Flax seeds

Sunflower seeds

Pumpkin seeds

Lemon juice

Pepper

Cooking Directions:

Chop the seeds in a food processor until they're the size of breadcrumbs.

Mash the avocado pump in a small bowl.

Mix with onion, pepper and lemon juice.
Blend well.

Serving Instructions, Variations and Tips:

Spread this dip on rice cakes, veggies or gluten-free crackers.

Thyme Butterbean Dip

Recipe Ingredients:

1 tablespoon of fresh thyme

1 tablespoon of lemon juice

¼ cup of olive oil

1 tin of cooked butterbeans

1 clove of garlic

Cooking Directions:

Place the ingredients in a blender or food processor and blend until smooth.

Serving Instructions, Variations and Tips:

If desired, season to taste with salt and pepper.

You can use 1 teaspoon of dry thyme in place of fresh thyme.

Gluten-free Corn Tortillas

Recipe Ingredients:

1 tablespoon of cooking oil

2/3 cup of warm water

1 cup of corn flour

1 pinch of Himalayan salt

Cooking Directions:

Combine the oil, salt and flour in a mixing bowl.

Slowly add water and mix. The dough must be firm.

Knead and work the dough.

Flour the counter and your hands and create the flat tortillas.

Pour the oil into a frying pan and warm.

Cook the tortillas until they're golden brown on each side.

Serving Instructions, Variations and Tips:

Serve with a gluten-free dip.

This recipe will serve 6.

Gluten-free Granola Crisp

Recipe Ingredients:

1/8 teaspoon of Himalayan salt

1 teaspoon of vanilla extract

3/4 cup of sunflower butter

3/4 cup of honey

1 cup of dried fruit

1 1/2 cups of seeds and nuts (roasted)

4 cups of brown rice crisp cereal

Cooking Directions:

Use wax paper to line a baking sheet.

Place the seeds, nuts and dried fruits in a food processor and grind into small chunks.

Melt the honey and butter in a large pan over medium-low heat.

Add the other ingredients and stir until everything is coated and evenly distributed.

Spread the granola into the pan and use a spatula to flatten it.

Serving Instructions, Variations and Tips:

If desired, substitute the sunflower butter with another nut butter variety.

Refrigerate for 2 hours before cutting the granola into bars.

Use wax paper to wrap or store them in an air-tight container in the refrigerator.

Conclusion

I hope you have enjoyed this healthy snack book and can recommend it to others!

If you liked this book, please check out my other books on Amazon.

Thank you.

Made in the USA
Coppell, TX
14 September 2022

83079338R00111